MANAGING YOUR OWN LEARNING

Other Books by
James R. Davis and Adelaide B. Davis

Effective Training Strategies: A Comprehensive Guide to Maximizing Learning in Organizations

Other Books by James R. Davis

Better Teaching, More Learning: Strategies for Success in Postsecondary Settings

Interdisciplinary Courses and Team Teaching: New Arrangements for Learning

MANAGING
YOUR OWN LEARNING

James R. Davis

Adelaide B. Davis

BK

BERRETT-KOEHLER PUBLISHERS, INC.
San Francisco

Berrett-Koehler Publishers, Inc.
450 Sansome Street, Suite 1200
San Francisco, CA 94111-3320
Tel: (415) 288-0260   Fax: (415) 362-2512   www.bkconnection.com

Ordering Information

Quantity sales. Special discounts are available on quantity purchases by corporations, associations, and others. For details, contact the "Special Sales Department" at the Berrett-Koehler address above.

Individual sales. Berrett-Koehler publications are available through most bookstores. They can also be ordered direct from Berrett-Koehler:
Tel: (800) 929-2929; Fax: (802) 864-7626; www.bkconnection.com

Orders for college textbook/course adoption use. Please contact Berrett-Koehler:
Tel: (800) 929-2929; Fax: (802) 864-7626.

Orders by U.S. trade bookstores and wholesalers. Please contact Publishers Group West, 1700 Fourth Street, Berkeley, CA 94710. Tel: (510) 528-1444; Fax: (510) 528-3444.

Printed in the United States of America
Printed on acid-free and recycled paper that is composed of 50% recovered fiber, including 10% post consumer waste.

Library of Congress Cataloging-in-Publication Data
Davis, James R., 1936–
    Managing your own learning / James R. Davis, Adelaide B. Davis. -- 1st ed.
      p. cm.
    Includes bibliographical references and index.
    ISBN 1-57675-067-1 (alk. paper)
    1. Adult learning.   2. Self-culture.   I. Davis, Adelaide B., 1949–. II. Title
LC5225.I 42 D38 2000
374--dc21
                                            99-058682

First Edition
06   05   04   03   02   01   00   10   9   8   7   6   5   4   3   2   1

Interior Design: Gopa Design   Proofreading: Carla Jupiter
Editing: Sarito Carol Neiman   Indexing: Paula C. Durbin-Westby
Production: Linda Jupiter, Jupiter Productions

Dedicated

to

Julianne and Scott
Lauren, Lindy, and Leah
Annalise
Marcela

CONTENTS

Part Three

MAXIMIZING LEARNING

ACKNOWLEDGMENTS

· ·

THERE IS SOME EVIDENCE that teaching a subject is a good way to learn it. This is especially true for learning about learning. Fortunately, we both have had the opportunity to teach students in a university setting, to study the literature on teaching and learning, and to reflect on our own teaching. Classes and workshops have provided for us an informal laboratory to experiment with different ways of teaching and learning. First and foremost, we would like to acknowledge our students—not only those in our formal classes but also the participants in our workshops in the United States and around the world. We have been very fortunate to learn about learning by encouraging bright and eager students, observing how they respond, listening to their feedback, and reflecting on what occurred.

We also want to acknowledge the help provided by Berrett-Koehler in transforming a mere idea for a manuscript into a book. After we wrote *Effective Training Strategies: A Comprehensive Guide to Maximizing Learning in Organizations*, a book primarily for facilitators, we stumbled on the idea of writing a book for participants in learning. Steven Piersanti, Berrett-Koehler's president, and the B-K staff grew excited about the idea and began to provide suggestions about how to define the audience and structure the book. Berrett-Koehler always provides a rigorous manuscript review process, but the reactions, insights, and suggestions of the readers for this manuscript were especially valuable. We want to acknowledge, therefore, the assistance of David Shapiro, Kendra Armer, Catherine Nowaski, Sara Jane Hope, and Katherine Weiser. The manuscript was revised extensively based on their suggestions. We also wish to acknowledge the work of Valerie Barth, senior editor, Elizabeth Swenson, production director, and Linda Jupiter of Jupiter Productions.

We appreciate the work of Mandy Anderson, graduate research assistant, for her excellent research about the Internet. We also want to thank Nancy Allen, Dean of Libraries at the University of Denver, and Deborah Grealy, Associate Professor and nontraditional programs librarian, for their generous consultation on libraries. Ray Ostlie, a graduate student and professional trainer, also provided insights as an informal reader of the manuscript. Sharon Irwin, Jim's administrative assistant, saw this book through from initial proposal to final manuscript, as she did with *Effective Training Strategies*. We have no idea, Sharon, how you can be so patient with so many changes in the manuscript.

Our own grandparents and parents are long gone from this earth, but we still hear their voices. The older we get the more we understand those cultures that revere the spirits of ancestors.

INTRODUCTION
. . . .
The Age of Perpetual Learning

FOR MANY OF US, living as we do in this fast-paced high-tech era, life is like trying to change a tire on a car while the car is still moving. It is a bizarre image, like something from a recurring dream—you can't possibly do what is expected, but you know your life depends on it. This is no dream. This is twenty-first-century reality. The only constant is change. Our only hope is perpetual learning.

Everyone today is either trying to get ahead, catch up, or keep from falling behind. Many people are trying to learn something just to survive—but learning is not fundamentally about survival, even though it often helps us to get through tough situations. Learning is the key to flourishing and prospering in this new era. Learning awakens our sensibilities, enables us to actualize our aspirations, and takes us places we never dreamed of going.

This book is for people who would like to improve the way they manage their learning. The key to doing that is learning more about learning so that you can get the most out of any learning you undertake. The goal is to become proficient at the process of learning itself.

1

Managing Your Own Learning is a book for a broad audience of learners:

- *Workforce learners* who have opportunities to participate in training and development programs in business, government, or not-for-profit organizations

- *Formal learners* enrolled in graduate or professional degree programs in colleges and universities or in continuing education programs

- *Part-time learners* in certificate or occupational programs in community colleges, proprietary trade schools, or the armed services

- *Independent learners* who are moving ahead on their own to learn what they want or need to know

- *Emerging learners* who may not even think of themselves as learners at this moment, but who have tremendous potential for learning

- *Awakening learners* who thought they had learned all they needed to know until they got that middle-of-the-night wake-up call

- *Recovering learners* who are trying to get beyond their previous bad experiences with learning so they can prosper in the new era

A NEW ERA
Not Just a New Millennium

The year 2000! We knew Y2K was coming. We read about it, heard about it, and got sick of hearing about it. Then it came. Is anything different? A lot of things are different, but they started being different long before the year 2000.

The cultural artifacts of a new era are now familiar and everywhere present: computers, lasers, robots, scanners, jet planes, bullet trains, color xerography, digital cameras, the Net, the Web. We are surrounded by high-order-of-magnitude change. Technological innovation drives much of the change, but we also experience other kinds of change: new organizational structures and management techniques, new means of production and service delivery, and a new global economy and communications network.

Call it what you will—the Information Age, the learning society, the cybernated world—this new era puts us all in a new situation with regard to our learning. It is the new era that is significant, not the new century or the new millennium. Time is arbitrary; events are real. The year 2000 on the Muslim calendar was 1420 A.H. On the traditional Chinese calendar it was 4690. What is different? Not the date, but the times and what the times demand of us—continuous learning.

The world we grew up in no longer exists. Everything is changing. Rapid change is a fact of life for people all over the world, in developed as well as developing nations. The entire globe has plunged into a new era of accelerated change with enormous consequences for learning. Older people in the workforce certainly feel this, but so do recent graduates. Whatever level of education they have just completed, they soon see that they were not exposed to learning they really need and learned many things that are already obsolete. Today, learning has a short shelf life.

Most of us today are under great pressure to learn new things. That pressure comes partly from the organizations where we work, but the broader source is the society in which we live. Furthermore, the new era demands of us real learning—not just going through the motions, seat time in a workshop, a diploma in hand or a certificate that says we were there. Credentials are still important, but what really counts is the learning behind and beyond the credentials. The bottom line is performance, and high-quality performance depends on perpetual learning.

PREDICTIONS THAT CAME TRUE
Looking Back on the Futurists

When was this new era born? Scholars began thinking about the new era long before it arrived. They read the signs of the times and began to predict a radically new future. Some people laughed at these predictions and made fun of the predictors, who came to be called *futurists.* In general, the predictions of the futurists have come true; if they were wrong, perhaps it was in underestimating both the rate and the scope of the changes.

According to an article in *Fortune Magazine,*[1] the world passed from the Industrial Age to the Information Age in 1991, the year that corporate spending on information technology surpassed corporate investment in manufacturing technologies (Stewart and Furth, 1994).[2] One of the leading futurists, Alvin Toffler, gives the new era a much earlier date: 1955, the beginning of a decade "that saw white-collar service workers outnumber blue-collar workers for the first time" (1980, 20).[3] Toffler was able to see that this new era was going to be upsetting. In an earlier work he called it *future shock,* "a time phenomenon, a product of the greatly accelerated rate of change in society" (1970, 13).[4] He compared it to the culture shock one experiences in traveling to another country, but with one important difference: you can't return home. It is not just change that causes future shock but the rate of change, what Toffler calls "the accelerative thrust" of change (1970, 20–34).[5]

The future described by the futurists (Toffler, 1972)[6] is not coming; it has arrived with full force. It doesn't matter when it began or what we call it; what we know for certain is that the new era is here. However much we may want to turn the clock back to another era, or slow the rate of change, we can't. Besides, there are many things most people like about the new era. We have no choice but to adapt. This is the Age of Perpetual Learning.

The chief characteristic of the Age of Perpetual Learning is rapid change. The real meaning of the year 2000 is that no one can survive without learning. Learning is driven both by necessity and passion. The key is to learn how to manage your own learning so that you can not only survive but thrive.

LEARNING ABOUT LEARNING
Using This Book

Although researchers know a great amount about learning processes after a fruitful century of investigation, most people remain relatively in the dark about how learning takes place. This is not the result of a conspiracy on the part of those who have provided our formal schooling; it is, rather, a matter of neglect. Few teachers or trainers believe their role includes sitting down with us to discuss the learning processes we are experiencing—even if they themselves had words to describe these processes, which they may not. Ironically, even after years of formal learning few people have a clear idea of what learning is or the many ways learning takes place.

Learning about learning is the organizing theme of this book. If you are able to learn the basics about learning, you should be able to maximize your learning in almost any setting. The structure of the book is simple and straightforward. In Part One you will learn how to assess your previous learning and build an action plan for further learning. You will also learn how to understand yourself as a learner and reframe your concept of learning. In Part Two you will find seven ways of learning presented, each in a separate chapter. At the end of each of those chapters you will find "Lessons Learned: Ten Things You Can Do to Maximize Your Learning." In Part Three you will find suggestions for how to use the seven ways of learning most effectively, how to use information sources such as bookstores, publishers, libraries, and the Internet, and how to find resources for continuing your learning.

Throughout this book there is an emphasis on taking responsibility for your learning, and maximizing your learning, in different settings. We call this overall process *managing your own learning*. Why did we pick the word *managing*? Definitions of management found in the classic textbooks include four interrelated functions: planning, organizing, motivating, and controlling. These four functions parallel what effective learners do.

- *Effective learners plan for learning.* They don't wait for learning opportunities to appear. They analyze carefully their needs for learning and aggressively seek out experiences that will meet those needs.

- *Effective learners organize their participation in learning.* They know how learning takes place and they think carefully about how they can best participate in order to maximize their own learning.

- *Effective learners motivate themselves to learn.* They understand themselves as learners and they know what they need to do to sustain their involvement long enough and strong enough to produce results.

- *Effective learners control their learning.* They seek feedback on how well they have learned. They know how to use information resources and how to find additional opportunities for learning.

In the factory model of mass education, the teacher was the manager. Although teachers and trainers still play important roles in *facilitating* learning, the ultimate responsibility for *managing* learning in this new era rests directly on the shoulders of the learner.

Most readers today skip around as they read. Recognizing this, we would like to provide some suggestions. If you already have a plan for learning and a good understanding of yourself as a learner, you may wish to plunge directly into the seven ways of learning in Part Two. These chapters can be read in any order, but we hope you will read enough of them to become knowledgeable about several ways of learning and to recognize that there are indeed different ways to learn. If you need help in locating resources for further learning after reading Chapter 1, you may want to turn directly to Chapter 13; you can read about using information resources, Chapter 12, at any time, and so forth. Although the arrangement of the chapters is intended to be logical, you can random access each chapter or special topic as you would with software, by using those old-fashioned search mechanisms called the Index and Table of Contents.

Most works of fiction have a central character. In this book *you* are the main character. We have provided headings, bulleted lists, and sections in italic to help you find important points. We want you to be an active learner as you read, and we encourage you to interact with the subject matter, look for main ideas, underline key points, and jot down reactions. Note especially the sections marked *Time Out*.

Time Out

Time Outs appear in each chapter to encourage you to think about what you are reading and connect it to your personal experience. Sometimes the Time Out provides a task for you to complete. We employ Time Outs to place you in an imagined situation, to underscore an important point, or to provide an example. Use them to give yourself time out to think about yourself and your learning.

This book has been written as a companion to our earlier work, *Effective Training Strategies: A Comprehensive Guide to Maximizing Learning in Organizations* (Davis and Davis, 1998).[7]

That book was developed for trainers, teachers, consultants, and others who facilitate learning in organizational settings. If you are a learning facilitator, or if you want examples from organizations and more technical detail on each of the seven ways of learning presented in this book, you should read *Effective Training Strategies: A Comprehensive Guide to Maximizing Learning in Organizations*. It is available in bookstores or through Berrett-Koehler Publishers.

Managing Your Own Learning provides you with a language you can use to describe your own efforts at learning and to discuss your learning experiences with others: students, colleagues, significant others, and those who serve as your teachers and facilitators. We believe there is an urgent need for dialogue about learning in this new era so that learning can be more focused and efficient and less happenstance and superficial. We invite you to help initiate and sustain this dialogue by sharing with others what you have learned from this book. If you wish to communicate with other readers around the world you can do so through the Consortium for Business Literacy, a group of publishers with whom Berrett-Koehler cooperates to facilitate dialogue among readers. You can also get from Berrett-Koehler a guide to use for group discussions about this book. See www.bkconnection.com or call (415) 288-0260. You can reach the authors through the publisher or at the University of Denver.

PART ONE

. . . .

Preparation for Learning

1

TAKING CHARGE

. . . .

Developing a Plan for Learning

Youth is wasted on the young, so it is said, and maybe education is, too. For most of us, at the stage in our lives when we had the most time for learning we also had the least appreciation for its benefits. Going to high school or college cultivates the mindset of blocks of years and plenty of time for learning. As people enter the workforce, develop personal relationships, and accumulate responsibilities, the need and desire for learning multiplies but the time available diminishes. We begin to sense that without a plan, we will never be able to learn all we want to learn.

When people take on a new job or project, or begin advanced studies, they often say, "There is going to be a steep learning curve." They are referring to a simple graph that plots the relationship of learning and time:

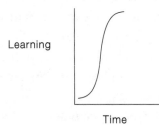

Learning

Time

11

Many people today are in situations that require significant amounts of new learning in a short period of time. Learning becomes a struggle: too much to learn and not enough time to learn it!

There are two good ways to meet the challenge of a steep learning curve. First, decide what to learn and make a plan for learning it. Second, when you get involved in some form of learning, make sure that you know how to learn so that you can get the most out of the learning experience. In this chapter you will learn how to develop a personal plan for learning. Managing your own learning begins with planning for learning.

Time Out

Reflect for a moment on your present situation. Can you identify learning you should undertake? Are you contemplating or are you already in the midst of new learning? Are you learning what you want to learn? How much time do you have for learning? Is there a pet project you continue to postpone? Would it help to have a plan?

THE BASELINE
Understanding Your Previous Learning

The place to begin in developing your plan for learning is with an honest analysis of your previous learning. Start with your formal education. Reflect on where you studied, the quality of the experience, the effort you put forth, and what you learned.

A useful way to analyze your formal education is to think about it in terms of proficiencies, conversancies, and specialties (Weingartner, 1992).[1] *Proficiencies* include such skills as reading, writing, speaking, and listening; interpersonal, group, or cross-cultural communication skills; critical thinking skills; quantitative skills in math, statistics, or computer science; foreign language skills; mechanical skills, or performance skills. These are the basic building blocks of further learning—the competencies you have now. They are things you can do.

Conversancies are the fields where you have a familiarity with basic information and ways of thinking. Think of them as areas where you can carry on an informed conversation within a general field or subject area. Knowing the main historical developments, major figures, key terminology, and central ideas in a field enables you to talk with others about that field and learn more within it. These fields include the basic subject areas we encounter in schools and colleges—humanities, social sciences, and sciences—but also professional and occupational conversancies: business, legal, medical, social service, educational, international, mechanical, agricultural, military, and technical. These are areas with which you have varying degrees of acquaintance.

In addition, you probably developed some *special expertise* in one or more academic, occupational, or professional areas where you studied in depth. In those areas you have developed more than a conversancy; you have gained the ability to find and understand information in that field, perform specialized tasks, or apply concepts from that field to practical situations. This special expertise might have been developed through an occupational specialization, college major, or through further study in graduate or professional school. These are areas where you have in-depth knowledge or well-developed, specialized abilities.

Your formal education is only part of the picture. Some people actually obtained very little from their formal education. They might have learned more through their *informal* education, through those things they learned on their own. Some people like to read, others travel, still others spend hours at the computer. Employees often have excellent opportunities for informal learning in organizational settings, as do volunteers. Many people have accumulated significant amounts of informal learning in areas unrelated to their jobs. Your previous learning consists of a blend of formal and informal learning.

PRIDE AND REGRETS
Assessing Strengths and Weaknesses

The important questions to ask as you try to establish your baseline are: What did you learn through formal schooling and on your own? What are your operational proficiencies, conversancies, and specialties? You can look at these as the strengths and weaknesses of your educational background, but a less threatening way to undertake this rigorous self-examination is to ask: What aspects of my formal and informal education do I take pride in, and what do I regret? In this way you have room to move ahead without blaming yourself or others. You can build on those aspects of your learning you take pride in, and remedy those areas about which you have regret. You are ready now to build a composite profile of your previous learning, a snapshot of yourself at this moment in time.

Time Out

Using the Planning Guide on the following page, fill in the first column with notes about your previous learning. Leave the other two columns blank for now. Think about your formal and informal learning, your proficiencies, conversancies, and specialties. Note areas where you take pride or have regrets.

PLANNING GUIDE

Previous Learning	Gaps	Desired Learning
Proficiencies:		Performance:
Conversancies:		Capacity:
Specialties:		Interests:
		Related Learning:

Action Plan:

PROJECTING LEARNING NEEDS
Knowing What You Need and Want to Know

Knowing where you are now is a starting point, but you also need to know where you want to go. What learning will be necessary for you to survive now and maintain yourself in the future? What will the job demand? These are questions about *performance*. Many training programs in organizations focus on performance improvement, the skills needed to do a specific job more effectively and efficiently. Improving performance is important, but you also need to think about the development of your *capacity*. What do you want to be able to do in three, five, or ten years? What will your job be like then, or what new job would you like to hold? What learning will be necessary for you to get there? Developing capacity is important, but you also need to examine your *interests*. What do you like to learn? Is there something you have been wanting to learn for a long time now, but for one reason or another haven't done it? Is there something you have a passion about learning? Do you have some dreams deferred?

The answers to your questions about performance, capacity, and interests need to be very specific. What exactly do you need to learn or want to learn?

To discover what kind of learning you will need for improving performance in your present job, consider the following guidelines.

- *Analyze the job.* Step back from the job and analyze what is involved in performing the job well. Develop hunches about what learning will be needed for the future. Think about what you need to know in order to be more effective in this job.

- *Talk about the job.* Discuss with supervisors, or others who hold this job, what directions it is likely to take and what new learning will be required. Identify what you can do to add value to the organization through this job.

- *Change the job.* Think about how to transform the job into a different job and decide what you need to learn to do that.

To improve your *capacity* for undertaking a new job, consider these guidelines:

- *Read about the job.* Most fields have trade magazines, news-letters, reports, and journals. What are the trends and new developments? What forecasts are being made about supply and demand? What will you need as a credential and what will you need to know?

- *Build networks.* Interview people who do this job or who are prospective employers. Find out what others believe you would need to learn to qualify for this job and perform it well.

- *Project the job into the future.* Imagine yourself or someone else doing this job in five years. What will they be doing and how will they be doing it? Think beyond what the job calls for now.

To identify your *interests,* consider these guidelines:

- *Note career paths you almost took but rejected.* What drew you to this learning in the first place, and what eventually turned you away from it? Do you have lingering interests in these areas?

- *Examine leisure-time interests.* Do you have hobbies or activities you enjoy more than anything else? What do you like to read or watch? Are these areas where you would like to learn more?

- *Recall favorite learning experiences.* What was your favorite subject, course, or workshop? What learning have you engaged in that was so much fun it hardly seemed like learning?

Generate information that will help you decide what you need to learn to be able to improve performance, develop capacity, or build on your interests. The goal is knowing what you need and want to know.

Your plan for learning also should include another important element: *related learning,* or learning beyond your field. It is important in an organizational context to identify the learning beyond your field that could have impact on your performance or capacity within your field. There are several reasons for branching out:

- *You need to communicate laterally, vertically, and outside the organization with other people.* Knowing enough to be conversant with the people with whom you work is important for good communication.

- *You need to be an effective team member.* You need to understand enough about the fields of other team members to work with them in a way that capitalizes on everyone's knowledge and skill.

- *You can gain new perspectives.* By acquiring knowledge and skills from outside your field, you can view your own field in a new way and gain insights about how to be more effective.

- *You can become more creative.* Today, most breakthroughs and new insights are interdisciplinary; that is, they come about by synthesizing information from two or more fields, or by using methods from one field to study phenomena in another field.

- *You can develop as a person.* Some learning is needed just for renewal, so that you can be a happier, more enthusiastic, and more interesting person.

Include in your plan for learning the related learning you will need outside your field so that you can communicate better, broaden your perspective, and be more creative and effective.

Time Out

Using the Planning Guide, provided on page 15, fill in the third column with notes about desired learning. Think about the learning you need for improved performance and expanded capacity, the learning that builds on your interests, and related learning that will broaden your outlook.

GAP ANALYSIS
Comparing Current Learning and Desired Learning

The next step in the personal planning process is to compare your findings about your current learning with your desired learning. No doubt there will be some gap, big or small, that needs to be closed by learning. Some of the previous learning you identified as matters of pride may put you in a good position for learning what you need to learn next. Some matters of regret may not be important at all in terms of what you need to know, but some regrets may be exactly the point of focus for closing the gap.

Be specific about the kind of learning that needs to take place to fill the gap. The learning may include knowledge or subject-matter information, but consider also such things as skills, including interpersonal skills, or the reworking of feelings and attitudes. As we will describe in Chapter 3, learning goes well beyond accumulating information. As you think about the gap, contemplate the many different kinds of learning that might fill it.

It will be tempting, as you think about the gap, to want to plug it with a program such as an MBA (Master's in Business Administration), a law degree, or a specific training program. You may eventually select more formal study as one means of filling the gap, but unless you have done a thorough gap analysis you won't know which program best meets your needs. Similarly, if you are already enrolled in further formal study, you should consider which aspects of the gap will be filled best by your current study and which will require other means of learning. A thorough gap analysis will help you analyze what specific learning is desired and what blend of formal and informal learning is most appropriate.

Time Out

Return to the Planning Guide on page 15 and make notes in the middle column to describe the gaps in your learning. Focus on specific learning outcomes described as new or enhanced proficiencies, conversancies, or specialties. Describe the learning needed, not the way of getting it.

GETTING WHERE YOU WANT TO GO
Developing an Action Plan

Now that you have a better idea about *what* you want to learn, begin to think about *how* you want to learn it. Be specific. What formal and informal learning opportunities will you seek? Where will you inquire about options? Who will you ask about opportunities? (See Chapter 13 for suggestions about finding opportunities for further learning.) If you are already enrolled in a formal training, certificate, or degree program, what choices can you make within that program—courses, projects, assignments—that will help you most to fill in the gaps in your learning? What steps must you take to carry out your plan?

Time Out

Return to the Planning Guide on page 15. At the bottom of the page, jot down notes about specific actions you will need to take to fill the gaps in your learning. Develop and prioritize the steps. What is the first step? What commitments of time and resources will you need to make?

Your personal plan for learning will grow out of your under-standing of your formal and informal education, your areas of pride and regret about previous learning, your analysis of your learning needs in an actual or potential employment situation, your assessment of your interests and passions, and your needs for learning outside your field. The key to your plan is an hon-est and realistic gap analysis—a sincere reflection on the dis-crepancies between your current learning and what you need or want to learn. A personal plan for learning provides the mecha-nism for focusing on specific goals. By pursuing your plan dili-gently you can prepare yourself for greater success in this new era. Managing your own learning begins with careful planning.

KNOWING YOURSELF
AS A LEARNER
. . . .
Estimating Your Potential

YOU CAN'T TEACH OLD DOGS NEW TRICKS, so they say. But if that is true, we all need to become new dogs fast, before we are replaced by quick-to-learn dogs. What makes us old dogs? Poor self-concept as a learner, fixed ideas about aptitudes and abilities, underestimating potential, too much emphasis on what we like and dislike—all that baggage we carry around from our previous experiences with learning. Attitudes about ourselves as learners are shaped over time—they are learned. In some cases they are positive and healthy, but in other instances they are dysfunctional and outmoded. If they are learned, they can be relearned.

The way you look at yourself as a learner can have an important impact on your learning. The next step in managing your own learning is to learn how to manage your perceptions of yourself as a learner. In this chapter you will learn how to paint a self-portrait of yourself as a learner and check it for accuracy as a likeness.

YOUR SELF-CONCEPT AS A LEARNER
Characteristics That Make a Difference

Listen to what people say about themselves as learners:
> I am not very motivated.
> I may be too old to learn this stuff.
> I never was a very good student—maybe about a C+.
> I have no aptitude for foreign languages.
> I am a right-brained learner.
> I am not very intelligent, especially when it comes to math.

As you listen to people describe themselves as learners, note how they use words that suggest fixed characteristics, as if they were describing a marble statue rather than a living, breathing, developing human being. Why is that?

When you become an adult you develop a general view of yourself called *self-concept*. This self-concept stretches across many areas of your life and includes your self-concept as a learner. The development of self-concept is a complex process, but takes place primarily by accumulating ideas about what others—parents, teachers, peers—think about you; that is, how you believe they regard you. You are likely to incorporate more strongly in your self-concept your beliefs about the perceptions of those whose opinions you value most.

Certain personal characteristics influence—notice that we did not say determine—how you learn, and these are the building blocks of your self-concept as a learner. Consider the following:

- *Age.* Age is important, but not in the sense of being too young or too old for learning. Age determines where you are in the developmental life span, which in turn influences what learning most interests you. Young adults in their mid-twenties who are trying to establish themselves in a career for the first time may have rather different interests from those of older adults in their mid-fifties (Levinson, 1996).[1] At each stage of life there are certain tasks that become the focus of our desire for learning (Havinghurst, 1972).[2] These developmental tasks influence what you want to learn, how intent you are on learning it, and how eager or hesitant you will be to engage in certain kinds of learning. Your self-concept as a learner is formed in part by where you are in the life cycle and how you regard your needs for learning at this point in your life. Transitions from one stage to the next are also important, and often require the support of learning (Sheehy, 1995).[3]

- *Intelligence.* Intelligence influences learning, but not in the sense of having it or lacking it. In the past, much emphasis has been put on general intelligence (Sternberg, 1985)[4] and the intelligence measured by I.Q. tests, but in recent years psychologists have broadened our understanding of intelligence to include multiple intelligences (Gardner, 1983).[5] These include linguistic, musical, logical, spatial, bodily and personal/interpersonal intelligences. Your self-concept as a learner is also shaped by how you view your intelligence. It is important to ask not only how much intelligence you have, but in what areas you have it.

- *Aptitude.* Aptitude is somewhat related to intelligence, but refers more directly to ability to learn. Some tests for entry into formal undergraduate and graduate programs test *general aptitude* (usually verbal and quantitative), but we also have *special aptitude* for specific types of learning such as using machine tools, flying airplanes, or learning foreign languages. Your self-concept as a learner is also shaped by your perceptions of your aptitudes, the things you are good at learning.

- *Achievement.* Achievement, which is sometimes confused with aptitude, refers to your actual current level of learning. Achievement includes what you have studied or worked with, and what level of proficiency you have attained. It refers to a specific area, so we usually say *achievement in. . . .* Your achievement levels also become part of your self-concept as a learner.

- *Motivation.* Motivation is also important in learning, but not as an inherent quality. Key aspects of a theory of motivation have been developed by Woldkowski (1993),[6] who notes that motivation comes into play before, during, and at the end of the learning process and relates not only to inner needs and how they are being met, but also the stimulation of the learning situation itself and the reinforcement we get out of learning. The amount of motivation you have varies with the learning to be undertaken, your need for that learning, and the specific situation where the learning will occur. Highly motivated people develop a sense of self-efficacy (Bandura, 1986),[7] an "I-can-do-it" attitude about reaching goals that gets reinforced when those goals are actually achieved. Our perceptions of our type and degree of motivation also become part of our self-concept as a learner.

- *Learning styles.* Most learning style theories focus on personality characteristics. Many of you will have encountered brain dominance theories and the personality types measured by the Myers-Briggs Inventory. Becoming more aware of your personality type helps you to discover the kinds of learning situations you prefer, and the way you may behave when you find yourself in different kinds of learning environments. Some learning style theories also focus on sensory modalities; that is, the strengths and preferences we have for auditory, visual, and tactile-kinesthetic learning. How you view your dominant personality traits and learning-style preferences also becomes part of your self-concept as a learner.

There are other characteristics you might consider as you examine your self-concept as a learner. Gender, social class, and ethnic background are also worth some reflection, but in general the characteristics listed above contribute most to our self-concept as learners.

....

Time Out

....

Find the first column on the Sketchpad on page 28 and begin to sketch in your current perceptions of those characteristics that make up your self-concept as a learner. How do you see yourself as a learner at this point in time?

....

Managing your attitudes about yourself as a learner begins with identifying your current perceptions.

CHALLENGING YOUR SELF-CONCEPT
Is It Accurate?

Here are three potential problems we all face with our self-concept as learners.

- We are often wrong in our perceptions, frequently under-estimating our potential.

- We place too much emphasis on unimportant characteristics while sometimes neglecting more important characteristics.

- We often attach a permanence to our perceptions that makes changing them difficult.

Time Out

Consider this example. A math teacher whose opinions you valued highly conveyed to you indirectly, in reviewing your work, that you were not very good at math. "Very good" may have meant, in her mind, as good as her three top students who learned quickly with minimal explanation. Disappointing your favorite teacher may have colored your perceptions but you came to believe it, made it a part of your self-concept as a learner, and even gave up the idea of careers that required math. Years later your self-concept as a learner still includes "not being very good at math." You treat that perception as cast in stone, as something that won't change. Could it be that the perception is distorted and that with proper instruction, a new setting, different motivations, and a better understanding of learning processes, you might be successful in learning some math-related skills? Can you think of other examples of self-concept formation where something like this might have happened to you?

SKETCHPAD FOR
SELF-PORTRAIT AS A LEARNER

Current Perceptions	Could Be Wrong?	Could Change?
Age/Stage:		
Intelligences:		
Aptitudes:		
Achievements:		
Motivations:		
Learning Styles:		

Before undertaking new learning, as part of your effort to implement your action plan, it can be important to reexamine thoroughly your self-concept as a learner. To do this, ask yourself these three questions:

- *Are some of my perceptions wrong?* Have I been thinking about age, intelligence, or motivation in the wrong way? Have I drawn false conclusions based on poor information from others and my own distorted perceptions? Am I underestimating my potential?

- *Have I placed too much emphasis on certain characteristics as opposed to others?* Do I, for example, give disproportionate weight to my learning style preferences, when in fact, aptitude, achievement, and types of intelligence may be much more important to my learning?

- *Do I view the elements of my self-concept as a learner as permanent, or am I able to modify some of them?* Should I continue to believe what I do about myself as a learner, or might I change some of my characteristics through new experiences?

Time Out

Go back to the Sketchpad, column 2, for your self-portrait and jot down your notes about how these self-concepts were formed and whether they are actually accurate. Then turn to column 3 and ask what elements of your self-concept might change if you were to have some new and different experiences with learning. What did you discover through this exercise?

RETOUCHING YOUR SELF-PORTRAIT
Estimating Your Potential for Learning

The characteristics we have described—age, intelligence, aptitude, achievement, motivation, and learning style—are important in learning. The big question is: How important? There may be some things you cannot learn because of inherent limitations. We all live within the boundaries of our capabilities, and our limitations are real. On the other hand, we often draw those boundaries unnecessarily tight and we have a tendency to under-estimate our potential. It may be more comfortable that way, but in this new era it is important to get beyond our limitations.

How does knowing yourself as a learner—drawing the most realistic self-portrait possible—help you in managing your learning?

- *Selecting learning experiences.* If you have made a realistic estimate of your potential, you are probably going to select appropriate learning situations. You will also be willing to undertake activities that test your self-concept as a learner. You won't be intimidated by your shortcomings and overwhelmed by having to operate outside your comfort zone. You will be realistic about challenges but optimistic about success.

- *Monitoring your participation.* You will be aware of what you like and what makes you uneasy, your strengths and your lim-itations. This will help you to understand why you respond as you do, and how you can participate more fully and more effectively in any kind of learning.

- *Being aware of effort needed.* All learning requires effort, but some learning requires more effort—sometimes because of the subject but more often because of your characteristics as a learner. You will know how much effort is needed—very little or very much—but you won't run from learning just because significant effort is required to compensate for limitations.

- *Being conscious of time needed.* Some learning, for certain learners, simply takes more time. Being conscious of your key characteristics as a learner helps you allocate appropriate amounts of time for your success.

Our view is that in recent years far too much emphasis has been placed on the importance of individual learner character-istics, particularly learning styles, in the mix of factors that influ-ence learning. Knowing yourself as a learner is important for the reasons just mentioned, but preoccupation with your characteristics and limitations as a learner may lead to a reluctance about learning that you cannot afford in this new era.

Time Out

Try to imagine the worst possible learning situation for you. It may be a two-hour lecture, a touchy-feely training group, an embarrassing role play in front of a large audience, a confusing exercise in problem solving, an ill-defined case study, or a wilderness challenge experience. What is the worst thing that can happen? Missing the point? Needing more time? Requiring more effort? Being embarrassed? Does any of that matter?

Knowing yourself as a learner is important, but let's avoid analysis paralysis. Climb out of your box, crawl out from under your desk, break out of your mental chains, and get out there and give it a try. There is a good chance you may have underestimated your potential. You may even be surprised to find out how badly formed and irrelevant your self-concept as a learner turns out to be.

The Age of Perpetual Learning requires that we become self-directed learners, aggressive learners, self-confident learners, and optimistic learners. In every situation that holds forth promise for learning, the question is not whether it is a perfect match for you, but whether you know how to manage yourself as a learner with insight, self-awareness, and courage.

REDEFINING LEARNING
. . . .
Examining Your Attitudes
About Learning

"HIRE FOR ATTITUDE, TRAIN FOR SKILLS!" This is a familiar slogan to those who work in human resource development. It suggests, of course, that it is easier to change people's skill levels than their attitudes, but the interesting point of the slogan is the importance placed on attitude. Attitude is important in much that we do, but it is especially important in learning.

The next step in managing your learning is to reexamine some of your ideas about learning. In this chapter you will be encouraged to reframe your definition of learning and develop up-to-date attitudes that will be adequate for the new era.

THE NEW IMPORTANCE OF LEARNING
No More Games

In the new era, learning is a serious matter. Business, government, and not-for-profit organizations are aware of the new importance of learning and are responding. Learning is being recognized as the key resource for continuous improvement and competitive advantage. Some organizations refer to themselves as *learning organizations,* some have started *corporate universities,* others are establishing *computer-based learning networks,* and a few have appointed *chief learning officers.* A new function in many organizations today is *knowledge management.*

Learning is no longer just an option; learning has become a way of life, a part of the culture of organizations. In most organizations today, everyone is teaching someone something somewhere. The question is: How fast and well will everyone learn? Learning is no longer a rare activity engaged in by an elite few. Perpetual learning is a necessity for everybody throughout the organization.

The new seriousness about learning in organizations sounds like a good thing, especially if you are ready to participate. Many people, however, have a fairly extensive history of not taking learning seriously. They played the game of getting by, meeting requirements with minimal effort, going through the motions of learning, and hiding and bluffing as necessary. They saw learning as a silly credentials game, a matter of jumping through hoops. They majored in deception and minored in excuses. Were you one of them?

Time-Out

All of us are perhaps some mixture of serious student and game player, part owl and part sloth. Take an honest walk back through your formal learning experiences and rate yourself on a scale of 1 to 10, where 10 is a serious learner. How would you score?

One of the first things to ask yourself as you explore your attitudes about learning is: What was your fundamental attitude about learning? If you carried into adulthood a game-player mentality from your school years, you probably recognize it now as a destructive form of self-deception and a key roadblock to effective learning.

If you are already a serious learner—one who takes responsibility, gets involved, meets deadlines, puts forth effort, and avoids making excuses—you already have the fundamental attitude needed for managing your own learning.

Learning and Change
Beyond Defensive Reasoning

Significant learning usually results in change in performance, capacity, or attitude. If we are not open to change, there is little reason to invest time, energy, and resources in learning. Change is the main product of learning and if we don't want to change, we probably do not want to learn either.

In a provocative article entitled "Teaching Smart People How to Learn," the internationally known scholar and consultant Chris Argyris (1991)[1] notes that many well-educated professionals are not very open to learning new things. The reason, he points out, is that learning involves risk and the potential for failure, and many people have arrived where they are by carefully avoiding both. Successful people often have developed a mindset about learning that Argyris calls *defensive reasoning*. They "screen out criticism," want to "put the blame on others," and are not very open "to examining their own role in the organization." The learning they are most interested in is the learning that will help them defend their established positions. Thus, learning feeds their process of rationalization. What they need instead, Argyris suggests, is "productive reasoning" that will break this closed loop and enable them to change and grow.

Time Out

On a scale of 1 to 10, how would you rate yourself on openness to change, where 10 is extremely open? Do you find yourself seeking information to support what you already believe, or are you willing to entertain new ideas that challenge your current way of thinking? A good test of this is to ask yourself which you want most: the credential for your resume, or the changed self that results from learning.

The article by Argyris is especially interesting because it suggests that people who have had the most education and career success may be the least open to what learning has to offer: the opportunity for change. "Smart people" as Argyris calls them, may need to ask themselves honestly whether they are truly open to additional learning and whether they welcome the changes that could occur.

An essential attitude to bring to any situation where learning could occur is openness to change.

LEARNING AND INFORMATION
Getting Beyond Facts

Learning is more than remembering facts. In the Information Age, our relationship to information has changed radically, and this in turn puts us in a new situation as learners. Three factors have had a dramatic effect on our understanding of learning in the Information Age: the explosion in the *amount* of information, the broadening of *access* to information, and the revolution in *packaging* information.

The information explosion hardly needs documentation. Now and then we read figures on how information doubles or triples every few months. In a fascinating critique of this information explosion, David Shenk (1997)[2] suggests in *Data Smog: Surviving the Information Glut,* that we are all faced now with serious information overload. Whether one perceives the amount of information today to be an advantage or threat, almost everyone agrees there is now a veritable deluge of information.

Equally impressive is the increased access to information. Libraries today provide networks of access through universal on-line cataloging systems for books and through powerful search mechanisms for articles listed in databases. Today, we can go to a database, enter key words for a topic, and several articles from a wide range of journals appear one after the other. The libraries themselves are also linked and, through the mechanism of inter-library loan, we can access most of the rapidly expanding store of information quickly and painlessly. The Internet is also important in increasing access to information. Information via the Internet comes through e-mail when people communicate directly with people, through Special Interest Groups (SIGs), through newsgroups or mailgroups, but most importantly through World Wide Web sites. Web pages (home pages) are now being established by companies, government agencies, not-for-profits, and individuals, and these sites often contain valuable, up-to-date information (Barrett, 1997, 34–58).[3] Access to this information is relatively easy through a host of Internet search and metasearch mechanisms.

Not only is there more accessible information, it is packaged in new user-friendly formats. Ease and variety in packaging information grows out of the ability to reduce all information, print or visual, moving or still, to digital formats. Because all kinds of data can be stored on computers in easily retrievable forms, information can be arranged and rearranged in different packages, including text, visuals, audio, and links to additional sources of information.

The explosion in the amount of information and easy access to it, combined with new capabilities for packaging it, has created a

*digital deluge. We now have a virtual Niagara Falls of informa-
tion at our disposal. Information is a dollar a ton and it is everywhere. The real question is: How do you draw a cup of water out
of Niagara Falls, and what do you do with it once you have it?*

In spite of the information explosion, many people continue
to define learning narrowly as remembering facts. In the previous era, information was scarce; having a lot of it was a virtue,
and memory was the key to learning.

Today we often have too much information, out-of-date information, or useless information. Note that information is not the
same thing as knowledge. Our big challenge today is turning
information into knowledge by developing our skills in locating
up-to-date information, validating and criticizing it, determining
what it means, deciding what to do with it, and learning how to
use it. Information has its place, but learning no longer needs to
be preoccupied, almost exclusively as it was in the past, with
transmitting and receiving information.

Time Out

To what extent have you grown up with the idea that education is
about facts and learning is about remembering?

ACTIVE PARTICIPATION
The Plague of Passive Learning

Children the world over learn at an early age to sit in their seats,
behave, and listen to the teacher. The lecture method, which
originated in the nineteenth-century German university, spread
around the world and came to dominate college and much high
school instruction. When learning is viewed as remembering

facts, the lecture method serves that purpose exquisitely. As the academic disciplines developed through the twentieth century, they provided a huge amount of information. Textbooks grew thicker and teachers felt they had more and more to cover. The more they covered, the less time there was for other methods of instruction. Students learned that their role in this educational process was to chew quietly and regurgitate on command.

Lecturing came to be the dominate paradigm for teaching and learning in the twentieth century. What it spread was a plague of passivity.

This arrangement is completely out of date for the Information Age, but continues in various forms with devastating consequences. What generations of students have really learned is that learning is basically receiving. Psychologists speak of "learned helplessness." The educational equivalent is "learned passivity." To some extent we have all learned this passivity from the educational system. We have learned that someone else is in charge of managing our learning.

There have been sharp criticisms of these arrangements for learning.

- Paulo Freire, the famous Brazilian educator exiled from his homeland after a military coup in 1964, called it the banking concept of education, by which "education thus becomes an act of depositing, in which the students are the depositories and the teacher is the depositor" (1987, 58).[4]

- Rudolph Weingartner, writing in *Undergraduate Education,* recounts a medieval tale that describes a wondrous device known as the "Funnel of Nuremberg" (*Nürnberg Trichter*), which has the remarkable quality of being able to pour knowledge into students' heads while they sleep (1992, 104–5).[5]

- Neil Postman and Charles Weingartner, the authors of *Teaching as a Subversive Activity,* note how the study of discrete subjects fosters the idea that once you have studied a subject you are immune and need not study it again, which they refer to ironically as the "Vaccination Theory of Education" (1969, 21).[6]

Wouldn't it be nice if we could get an education by having someone make a deposit in our account, pour it in our ear, or give us an injection? Learning in the new era requires that we cast off the old habit of passivity and take on with renewed vigor the role of active participant.

....

Time-Out

....

Can you provide examples of how you learned to be a passive learner? Were you good at regurgitating facts? Are you comfortable with the role of active participant?

....

REFRAMING YOUR DEFINITION OF LEARNING
No One Best Way

For some reason, educators are especially prone to the bandwagon trap. Schools become captives of fads, and organizations buy into quick-fix training solutions. In truth, there is no one best way of learning. There are many ways to learn, not just one. We would like to offer a broad definition of learning:

> *Learning is that varied set of processes whereby individuals and groups of individuals acquire knowledge or skill, change attitudes, become better informed about something familiar, or discover, inquire about, or become aware of something new.*

> *Learning involves the development of intellectual and emotional capacities—the ability to think, to build skills,*

to find and solve problems, to be creative, to manage
emotions, to change attitudes, to perform, and to learn
from experience. In organizational settings, learning
usually also involves a change in performance, based
on new understanding—a better, faster, smoother, more
reasonable way of doing something, or at least an
improved capacity for doing so.

In the Information Age, learning is not the accumulation of mis-
cellaneous bits of information, but the subtle set of skills involved
in knowing what to do with information. It is the ability to eval-
uate, synthesize and apply information. The purpose of learning
is not just to inform but to transform. The goal is not just to cover
material but uncover ideas and feelings. Above all, learning is
not a spectator sport!

The following statements are especially useful for describing
adult learning in the Information Age, and are presented as
corollaries to our basic definition of learning.

- *Learning is an ongoing process.* Learning has many beginnings
  but no end. One only becomes relatively better at certain skills
  and abilities, only relatively more informed, only relatively
  more sophisticated at intellectual operations.

- *Learning has subject-matter content, but the subject is usually*
  the means not the end of learning. Content is not irrelevant,
  but neither is it the main goal anymore. Content is the vehicle for learning, the medium through which learning occurs.

- *Learning is self-motivated.* Learning takes place best when the
  learner wants and needs to learn. Self-motivation puts an end
  to all the student-teacher-trainer games about "how much am
  I supposed to do" and "how good is this supposed to be."

- *Learning is aggressively self-directed.* Although many people
  can provide guidance, particularly those who know about learning processes, the learner needs to select, monitor, and pursue
  vigorously the scope, depth, and type of learning needed.

- *Learning is dialogical.* Learning takes place through conversation with other people, with books and materials, and with the self. True dialogue involves self-examination by listening to other voices and assimilating, accommodating, and adjusting to what they say.

- *Learning involves constructing meaning.* Knowledge is produced only when information takes on meaning. The learner needs to be actively involved in constructing personal answers to relevant questions.

- *Learning is perceived as useful.* Some learning has no direct application and is undertaken to satisfy curiosity or for amusement, but most learning is useful someday, somewhere, sometimes even the next day.

- *Learning changes the self.* Only those things that truly touch, change, and become absorbed into the self are really learned.

- *Learning is used responsibly.* Because knowledge is a powerful resource in the new era, the results of learning should be used for constructive purposes.

Time-Out

Which aspects of this definition of learning, with its accompanying corollaries, appeal to you most? Viewed in this way, does learning appear more natural, functional, and attractive? Does this appear to be a satisfactory way of reframing the definition of learning? Do these ideas inspire you to want to be more effective at managing your own learning?

The attitudes we bring to an opportunity for learning, and the way we define learning, greatly affect what we learn. The paradox is this: Our attitudes are learned from others, but only we can change them. In a sense, we are the product of the experiences we have had, the system in which we have been edu-

cated, and the society in which we have lived. In that sense, we
are not to blame. Nor are we to blame when everything around
us changes. But society has changed, and the new era requires
of us new attitudes about learning.

*In the Information Age, we need to recognize that learning is a
serious business. Learning is not just remembering information.
Learning requires active participation. We need to broaden our
definition of learning and become adept at several ways of learning. In Part Two you will learn about how to participate effectively in seven ways of learning. This is an essential aspect of
managing your own learning.*

PART TWO

. . . .

Seven Ways of Learning

INTRODUCTION TO THE
SEVEN WAYS OF LEARNING

· ·

PART TWO CONTAINS SEPARATE CHAPTERS on seven different ways of learning. Each way of learning brings about different outcomes and, therefore, has different purposes. By reading these chapters you will be able to

- identify when these ways of learning are being used.

- know more about how learning takes place within the framework of each way of learning.

- understand your role as participant and what you can do to maximize your learning.

LEARNING THEORIES
Foundations of Effective Learning

People tend to confuse learning styles and learning theories. In Chapter 2 we mentioned learning styles as one of the sets of characteristics, along with several others, that are important in forming your self-concept as a learner. In the last fifteen years there has been a frenzy of interest in learning styles, and this has heightened our awareness of individual differences in learners. Although this was an awareness that needed to be cultivated, putting the spotlight on learning styles has relegated to the shadows the fundamental theories of learning that guide the activities through which all people can learn.

It is very important to distinguish the difference between learning theories and learning styles. Learning styles are the ideas about how personality differences and certain sensory capacities lead to preferences for particular ways of learning. Learning style is but one of the many human characteristics that are important in learning. Learning theories, on the other hand, are the basic theories about how learning takes place for people in general. They are the sound, well-researched theories of learning that support the seven ways of learning presented in the chapters of Part Two of this book. Understanding and grasping the importance of these theories is essential for the process of managing your own learning.

During the last century, scholars have greatly expanded our knowledge about learning and have provided many useful theories about how people learn. The theories are different from each other because they describe different ways of learning. For example, learning a set of skills through a very carefully developed sequence of steps is quite different from learning new attitudes through a group process. Similarly, learning to attend to, process, and remember information from a presentation is different from the holistic learning that comes through having and reflecting on a new experience. Each of these different ways of learning is supported by theory.

Don't be put off by the word *theory*. A theory is just a comprehensive explanation that accounts for facts and processes. A good theory makes a convincing argument for how things work. A famous saying attributed to Kurt Lewin, the well-known theorist of group behavior, tells us, "Nothing is as practical as a good theory" (Morrow, 1969).[1] We agree. Theories help us to see more clearly things that otherwise would be a blur.

Some people are inclined to say, "Theories are just theories; real life is different." Some theories are like that, of course, but many theories have been tested extensively. Theories that have been tested carefully can be called *well-established theories.* Fortunately, we now have a number of useful, well-established learning theories. Learning theories are valuable because, when used effectively, they can describe a particular way of learning, establish what role facilitators should play, clarify what learners should be doing, organize the communication process, and maximize outcomes.

After conducting a great amount of research on learning, and after giving significant thought to how to organize and categorize various ways of learning, we have settled on seven ways of learning that encompass most of the kinds of learning you might need or encounter. You should develop a working knowledge of these seven ways of learning. This includes a basic understanding of how each way of learning functions, what outcomes it best produces, and what you can do to maximize your own learning when you are learning in that way.

The seven ways of learning presented in the chapters in Part Two are introduced below through a series of questions. (Davis and Davis, 1998, 91–92).[2] The questions will help you to identify each of the seven ways of learning and will enable you to distinguish one way of learning from another. This introduction will also help you decide which chapters you want to read next or focus on most.

1. *Learning New Skills: Behavioral Learning.* Does this learning involve a skill? Is this something concrete and observable? Is it a routine (though not necessarily easy) set of mental or physical operations that can be tested or observed? Is this a task that you can learn to do or learn to do better?

2. *Learning From Presentations: Cognitive Learning.* Does this learning involve information? Does it involve new ideas,

new terminology, or useful theories? Does it require understanding of how something works or functions? Is this information that might be presented through an explanation? Is it
possible to identify key concepts, main ideas, or points to be
understood and remembered?

3. *Learning to Think: Inquiry Learning.* Does this learning
focus on thinking? Does it involve criticizing information, evaluating arguments and evidence, or reasoning to conclusions?
Does this learning involve creative thinking—actually producing unusual but relevant new ideas? Does it involve appre-
ciating how other people think?

4. *Learning to Solve Problems and Make Decisions: Using
Mental Models for Learning.* Does this involve learning
how to find and define problems, how to generate solutions,
and how to evaluate and choose among solutions? Does this
learning require that you deal with issues where you need to
make choices, weigh the value of different options, and predict outcomes as probabilities?

5. *Learning in Groups: Collaborative Learning.* Does this
learning involve changing opinions, attitudes, and beliefs?
Does it deal with feelings? Does it build interpersonal speaking and listening skills? Does it cultivate empathy? Is teamwork or collaboration being addressed here?

6. *Improving Performance: Learning Through Virtual
Realities.* Is this a kind of learning that needs to be practiced
in a safe environment? Does this learning involve activities
that could cause damage, expense, or even loss of life? Will
you feel more confident and be more competent if you have
been able to work first in a simulated environment before
going into the real world?

7. *Learning From Experience: Holistic Learning.* Is this a
kind of learning that bubbles up from experience? Is this the
holistic learning that occurs when you go out and get
immersed in a new experience? Could you learn something
more from this experience if you had a chance to reflect on it
and construct meaning from it? Is there potential here for
learning to see something in a new way?

Sometimes you will have the chance to choose learning opportunities that are exactly what you want. At other times you will find yourself in learning situations that are demanding, uncomfortable, and not what you prefer. In the new era, there are simply many things one *must* learn, and sometimes you have little choice, no place to hide. Some people hate to be placed in groups, some are bored with cases, others panic when faced with problem solving. The question is not whether you will like it. The more important question is: Can you profit? This is why learning about learning is so important. You need to be able to maximize your learning in any situation.

The First Way of Learning

LEARNING NEW SKILLS

. . . .

Behavioral Learning

SOMETIMES WHEN WE ARE LEARNING A NEW SKILL we want to say, "Slow down, I need to take this a step at a time." Not a bad instinct! The step-by-step approach is the essence of behavioral learning.

Most jobs require skills. Some skills involve physical movements and are what psychologists call *psychomotor skills*. Other skills involve the ability to make routine calculations or follow procedures. They are called *cognitive skills* because they require mental effort. Sometimes psychomotor and cognitive skills are combined. Skills can be simple or complex. A skill is a patterned set of operations requiring routine—though not necessarily easy—physical activity, mental activity, or both.

. . . .

Time Out

. . . .

You are standing at the check-in counter for Flight 4024. The process appears to be taking much longer than it should, and you begin to make observations. The employee behind the counter, whose name tag reads "Leonard," is using the index finger, hunt-

and-peck typing technique. A lot of information is being entered, but then canceled and re-entered. The four tickets for your family are spread across the counter, picked up, reshuffled, and spread out again. You have been asked the routine security questions twice, and now you are being asked for your I.D. for the second time. You are straining to read the baggage tags to see if they indicate the right city. What is wrong with this picture? You conclude that Leonard's basic skills for this job are not in place. You start to wonder about the pilot.

MOVING FROM RAW BEHAVIOR TO SKILLS
Shaping

Psychologists first learned about behavioral learning through a series of clever experiments performed on animals in laboratory settings. Just as new medicines are first tested on animals, so also were some of the earliest theories of learning. The pioneer in this field was B.F. Skinner (1953[1], 1974[2]) who picked up on an idea from E.L. Thorndike—behavior is affected by consequences—and elaborated it into one of the first learning theories. It is still valuable and is used widely in training designed to build skills. If you understand the theory, you can learn more from trainers who use it. You can also use it to learn new skills on your own.

There is no better way of understanding behavioral learning than to return to those early laboratory experiments (Keller, 1969).[3] Suppose that the objective is to train a pigeon to turn clockwise in a complete circle. First the trainer must describe the learning outcome in terms of observable behavior. In this instance, turning circles is comparable to the skills to be learned in training, such as learning how to check in passengers accurately and efficiently. Next, the pigeon is put into a specially designed box and observed to see what it can do. (Maybe it already knows how to turn circles.) Trainers call this step *measuring present performance level*. If you are working alone, this step involves asking yourself what part of the skill, if any, you can do now. Assume that the pigeon does not turn circles, but only walks around randomly poking its beak into every nook and cranny of the box. How does the trainer move the pigeon from raw behavior to skills?

The answer is to break the objective into a series of small steps called *tasks*. Thus when the pigeon makes its first move—it may simply shift its weight to the right foot—it is reinforced with food dropped into the box at just the right moment through a device controlled by the trainer. Next the pigeon steps to the right and leans to the right. Accidental? No problem. More food appears. Then the pigeon takes two steps to the right and twists its neck back and to the right. Food drops into the tray again. The whole process is called *shaping,* and it continues one step building on another until the objective is attained.

Time-Out

Recall a skill you have learned, or think of one you would like to learn. Does learning it parallel the process just described? Is it the kind of learning that could be broken into steps? Could Leonard learn the skills he needs this way? We hope Leonard will get further training but if not, he probably could teach himself the skills he needs through the behavioral way of learning.

SETTING GOALS
Behavioral Objectives

When behavioral learning is being used for teaching skills it is necessary, first of all, to get very specific about outcomes, often called *behavioral objectives*. Most trainers who use behavioral learning have these objectives spelled out, usually in writing, and usually trainers will share these with the participants. If not, you should ask for the behavioral objectives. These will help you to get a clear picture of what you should be able to do as a result of the training. Behavioral objectives should use very specific language, such as *to construct, to list, to arrange,* as opposed to vague words such as *to understand* or *to appreciate* (Mager, 1962).[4] If you are using behavioral learning to teach yourself a new set of skills—and you can do this—the first step is to become very clear about what you will be able to *do* when you have learned what you want to learn.

Time Out

A behavioral objective for this chapter would be: After reading this chapter you will be able to identify and describe the key elements of behavioral learning, including *behavioral objectives, present performance level, task analysis, feedback,* and *shaping.* In addition, you will be able to explain how behavioral learning is the foundation for certain types of computer-assisted instruction and for instructional design.

BEGINNING IN THE BEGINNING
Present Performance Level

Sometimes trainers will give you a part of the task to try, just to see how well you can do it before you are given any training. This is done to establish your *learning baseline*. In its written form this is often called a *pretest*. Trainers might start you in the beginning or in the middle of the task, just to get a feel for what you can do. This raises an interesting question: Where is the beginning? If you can breeze through the first five steps perfectly, the chances are good that for you, step one is not the beginning. On the other hand, if step one is posing problems for you, that is not the beginning either. You may need to develop some *prerequisite* skills.

Time Out

Leonard lacks the keyboard skills that are a prerequisite for using the computer as a word processor. Although the job description may not call specifically for keyboard skills, no one, including Leonard, is going to be able to use the computer effectively without keyboard skills. Fortunately, there are simple programs for this skill that also use behavioral learning.

If you start a task and realize you do not have the "right stuff" for success, just back up a bit and find out what prerequisite skills you need before proceeding with the plan for training. You should have no embarrassment about lacking prerequisite skills; the embarrassment comes only if you don't develop them.

STEP BY STEP
Task Analysis

Knowing your destination is one thing; getting there is another. An objective is seldom achieved in one leap: jumping barrels on a motorcycle has its perils. Behavioral learning proceeds in steps. Most trainers using behavioral learning put considerable effort into breaking the training into small steps, a process known as *task analysis* (Davis, et. al., 1974).[5] By analyzing the skill very carefully, by watching it performed, and by breaking it into its component parts and then sequencing these parts as tasks and subtasks, trainers are able to make learning more efficient and effective. This is no easy job. It requires a special eye and is a skill in itself. Trainers may or may not be good performers of the task—some figure skating coaches do not skate well themselves—but they must be proficient in analyzing the skill so that it can be taught systematically.

If the task analysis has been done carefully, and with sufficient detail, your learning should follow a smooth progression. Look for the tasks and subtasks. Also be alert for something missing. The tendency of teachers and trainers all over the world is to go too fast and to skip important steps. We learn to walk before we run, and we learn to walk with baby steps. Ask yourself: Did I miss something here? Some subtasks are more difficult and may require more practice before moving on. If you appear to be stuck, either a step is missing or you need more time to master a difficult subtask. The shaping process can break down at any step. Remember, shaping the learning through small steps is the key to behavioral learning.

If you are using behavioral theory to design your own learning, doing a task analysis is essential. Ask yourself what you need to learn first, then second, and so forth. Be careful not to skip steps and be sure to make the steps small.

Time Out

Have you discovered the steps in this chapter? We gave you an overview of the shaping process but now we are introducing you step by step to the key building blocks of behavioral learning: *objectives, present performance level, task analysis,* and *feedback.* A task analysis suggests that these are the steps and there is a logical order to them.

Sometimes you will be given the steps as you go along through the training; at other times the whole process or several parts of the process will be demonstrated. These demonstrations are called *modeling* (Bandura, 1969).[6] If the skill is demonstrated, you may find it valuable to watch closely and look for the steps and the progression of tasks. A novice watching an Olympic diver will not be able to perform a perfect dive by watching, but some overall understanding of the learning can be gained as well as an awareness of what the skill looks like when it is being performed well. The classic studies reported by Bandura on *modeling, vicarious learning,* and *imitation* suggest that learners who watch a task being performed actually benefit just from watching.

Time Out

Let's hope Leonard gets some help in analyzing and organizing the different parts of his job. The parts can then be broken into tasks and subtasks so that Leonard can learn them more efficiently. Leonard would profit from watching someone who does his job expertly, but he will also need to develop, one by one, the skills that the expert demonstrates proficiently.

REWARDING YOURSELF FOR GOOD BEHAVIOR
Feedback

The essence of behavioral learning, however, is action—having the opportunity to practice the skill under guidance. The learner tries something and the trainer provides feedback. Recall the pigeon learning to turn in clockwise circles in the laboratory. The pigeon tries something, actually many things, but only certain things bring food. The right moves bring positive consequences. It is at this crucial moment, when a specific action gets linked with a particular consequence, that learning occurs. The process of linking behavior to consequences is called *reinforcement*. In training this is usually called *feedback*.

Feedback is of two types: rewards and punishments. Behavior that immediately proceeds a reward is likely to be repeated; hence a reward is often referred to as a *positive reinforcer*. Positive reinforcers are anything an individual is willing to put forth effort to obtain. Punishments, on the other hand, are those things that an individual is willing to work hard to avoid. For a consequence to work as a positive reinforcer, it must be satisfying to that particular individual. Naturally, there will be considerable variation in tastes. What works for some doesn't work for others.

Probably the most important feedback in learning a skill is the *internal reward* that comes from performing the skill correctly. Correct performance alone, therefore, will often establish the skill if you are given feedback on what correct performance is. This is called *knowledge of results*. Often you will get feedback from the equipment, process, or interaction taking place. But at other times some *external reward* is needed, particularly in the early phases of working through tasks and subtasks. Although it may appear childish, most of us like and will work hard for very simple forms of positive reinforcement, such as praise, attention, recognition, good scores or encouraging comments on tests, free time, various types of food, points, trophies, certificates, awards, and promotions or pay increases. Positive reinforcers are anything that might convey approval or generate satisfaction. In most training this involves well-timed knowledge of results coupled with praise.

Punishment usually takes on the form of *negative reinforcement,* the setting of conditions we will work hard to avoid. Like positive reinforcement it can be used intentionally or can occur naturally. Most of us will try to avoid such things as poor performance, required repetition of the task, working longer on the task, failing a test or checkpoint, critical remarks on papers or tests, reprimand or embarrassment, demotion, pay cut, or losing one's job. All of these conditions serve as threats, and we will work hard to keep them from happening to us. Trainers usually like to stress positive reinforcement, but a lot of learning still occurs through avoidance of threats, spoken or unspoken. Punishment—the actual application of threats similar to these—is seldom used, except when you may be doing something that poses a risk to yourself or others.

Because feedback is so important to behavioral learning, it needs to be strong and well timed, which means as close as possible to the occurrence of a well-performed task. If you aren't getting the feedback you need, if it isn't clear enough or appropriately timed, you need to ask for it. You need feedback at each step, not just at the end. If you are trying to learn something on your own, you still need to get feedback, to ask yourself how you are doing and set little rewards for yourself for getting things right. It may seem like you are playing a game with yourself—getting a snack or giving yourself free time after completing an important task or subtask—but this is what makes behavioral learning work. From the pigeon's point of view, no food, no circles.

Time Out

How well do you understand behavioral learning so far? It consists of certain building blocks, right? Can you name them? Can you put them in logical order? If you said, *objectives, present performance level, task analysis,* and *feedback,* you've got it. Nice work! If not, go back and review. Can you describe in a sentence or two how each building block works? If so, you already have the main ideas of this chapter. Take a five-minute break. Think about what Leonard needs to do to win the Employee of the Month award.

Behavioral learning functions as a total system. All of the building blocks must be in place to make it work. Behavioral objectives are fine, but to achieve them you also need task analysis and well-timed feedback. Watch for missing pieces. For many things you want to learn you can probably do an adequate task analysis, but you still need to get feedback on how you are doing at each step for the shaping process to work.

FRAME BY FRAME
Computer-Assisted Instruction

In 1961, B.F. Skinner published an article in the *Harvard Educational Review* entitled "Why We Need Teaching Machines."[7] It took several years for the hardware, software, and learning technology to come together, but programs that draw on the behavioral way of learning are now readily available on computers. *Computer-assisted instruction* (CAI), sometimes known as drill-and-practice software, is built on behavioral learning theory although the connection is not always made.

Consider how it works. Learning outcomes are established as a basis for the software design (behavioral objectives). Information is displayed on the screen in sequential steps called *frames* (task analysis). On each screen, the information contains embedded prompts or clues along with questions that call for a response. When you respond, the computer reads your choice and replies with either confirmation of the right answer (knowledge of results) accompanied with appropriate praise (reinforcement), or with suggestions about how to get the right answer (feedback). Because a computer can be programmed, it can be ready for a range of responses from you and will make decisions about the reply. Several different replies are possible, including where to look for help, how to try again, or what to do to correct something that went wrong. Some CAI incorporates an *expert system* that catalogs and analyzes your responses and offers help based on that analysis (Graham, 1986).[8] The expert system can direct you back for review or forward for more challenging material. It is even possible now to move beyond frame-oriented CAI to *generative* CAI (McCann, 1981).[9] The computer generates questions as it goes, based on what it "knows" about the subject matter and you as a learner. By using sophisticated algorithmic descriptions of classes of problems, and rating your performance in solving them, it produces customized lesson material for you.

A more recent application of behavioral learning theory to computers is in the linking of visual materials to CAI. A CD-ROM can store thousands of frames of visual information including slides, sections of films, videotapes and graphics, as well as large libraries of text. Real images, not just computer graphics, appear on the screen. It is possible to jump forward and back through this information very rapidly and with precise control. For example, you can move in and out of the text or graphics to seek definitions, to review information previously presented, or to seek related visual material on a topic or subtopic. This puts you in charge and enables you to pace your learning at the speed that is best for you, and to take the time needed with various steps. Similar arrangements using the behavioral way of learning are also being made available on websites.

Time Out

Leonard could profit greatly from spending several hours with any of several available software programs used to teach basic keyboard skills. You begin by putting all ten fingers in the home position, and the program teaches you step by step where all the letters and symbols are on the keyboard and which fingers to use to strike them. The software helps you learn and practice at your own speed. Perhaps Leonard's company also has or is developing software on the ABCs of the check-in process. If there is a skill you need to learn, including how to design software, you shouldn't be surprised today to find software designed to help you learn it quickly.

COURSES THAT USE BEHAVIORAL LEARNING
Instructional Design

The ultimate application of the behavioral way of learning is in large-scale instructional systems that control as many of the components of the learning process as possible: objectives, tasks, written materials, visuals reinforcement, and tests. The goal of such courses is to guide the learning process from beginning to end, using behavioral principles. Such efforts are sometimes referred to as *instructional design.*

A specific kind of instructional design known as Personalized System of Instruction (PSI) was developed at the University of Arizona by Fred Keller, one of B.F. Skinner's graduate students (1968).[10] A PSI course can have many variations, and the name is seldom used today, but you can look for courses that use the principles. These courses usually involve a precise set of objectives and a series of self-paced learning modules and materials—booklets, manuals, laboratory or workstation activities, presentations, demonstrations, software, films, videotapes, and audiotapes. Many organizations have developed systematically designed courses of instruction that they use in training and development. Some of these courses are available as software, some are on the Internet as Web-based courses, and others are distributed internally on the organization's intranet. Many Web-based courses are also available commercially. Watch for courses that use instructional design and notice how they use the behavioral way of learning.

Time Out

The problems Leonard is having checking in passengers for Flight 4024 could be avoided through systematic skill development using the behavioral way of learning. A course based on instructional design would be wonderful, as would software for teaching keyboard skills. With a little help from a concerned supervisor, Leonard could identify the skills he needs to develop, break them into steps, attempt each step, and seek feedback.

You can use the shaping process effectively to manage your learning of skills. You may or may not like the behavioral way of learning, but for building certain skills it may be the quickest and most effective way to learn. Give yourself a pat on the back for completing this chapter, and if you use this way of learning to learn new skills next week, give yourself a big hug.

LESSONS LEARNED
Ten Things You Can Do to Maximize Your Learning

1. Look for or ask for clearly stated behavioral objectives.

2. Take a pretest or establish a baseline of what you already know.

3. Look for steps—the tasks and subtasks that take you to the objective.

4. If necessary, do your own task analysis to break your learning into steps.

5. Request a demonstration by an expert at performing the skill.

6. Seek timely feedback to get knowledge of results.

7. Expect reinforcement or provide it for yourself.

8. Watch for behavioral principles in computer-assisted instruction and use what you know to learn from it efficiently.

9. Search for software that uses behavioral learning.

10. Find self-paced or Web-based courses that use instructional design principles.

The Second Way of Learning

LEARNING FROM PRESENTATIONS
· ·

Cognitive Learning

Stand outside of lecture halls and listen to students as they come pouring through the doors, and you will often hear them saying, " . . . that was so boring . . . I had no idea what was going on in there today . . . besides, who's going to remember all that stuff." Every student or participant in training knows from prior experience that a presentation can be brilliant or dull, involving or boring, enlightening or deadly. The same can be said for books, articles, training manuals, and other modes of presenting information. What makes it so? Some would say the personality of the author or presenter, the content, or the visuals. In fact, a lot has to do with the format of the presentation and the way it matches or fails to match up with how human beings are designed to attend to, process, and remember information. The response of the learner is also important.

Time Out

You are one of two hundred managers and supervisors invited to a presentation next week by the chief executive officer (CEO) of your company. The topic is quarterly performance and near-range and long-term goals. You remember your previous experience with lectures and presentations in college and you are already bored just thinking about it. Listening to presentations doesn't fit your preferred learning style. You also know that this is no ceremonial speech, not a symbolic exercise of rhetoric and platitudes, but a serious effort to communicate company performance and goals. How can you learn what you need to learn from this presentation?

Many jobs require that we understand important facts, comprehend processes, and remember essential details. The information we need today often involves technical language, difficult concepts, and subtle relationships among ideas. Information is presented in many modes—through lectures and explanations, text on computer screens, training manuals, reports, booklets, books, and professional journals. Learning from these various presentation modes requires that we attend to, process, and remember information. This is cognitive learning.

Cognitive psychology has no B.F. Skinner, no single figure who can be said to be its founder or foremost spokesperson. Between 1950 and 1980 a whole new subfield of psychology was created by researchers who wanted to know what goes on in the mind when people process information (Gardner, 1985).[1] Drawing on the emerging fields of linguistics and computer science, cognitive psychologists devised clever experiments and built creative models to describe human information processing (Neisser, 1967).[2] Collectively their work is known as *cognitive learning theory*.

LISTENING AND WATCHING
A Basic Information Processing Model

The way we listen and watch has been investigated extensively by cognitive psychologists. Early in their research, they reached agreement on the outlines of a basic information processing model (Atkinson and Shiffran, 1968).[3]

According to this model, information enters through any of the five senses and impinges on a *sensory register*. *Filters* are activated and let pass or screen out what we will give our attention to, based on interest or necessity. The main features of the information are *analyzed* and *encoded*. They are held in *short-term memory* for a few seconds while a decision is made about what to do—respond directly, think about them, integrate them with old information, or store them in *long-term memory*. Sometimes the new information requires a search for old information. Although the model is complex, there appears to be general agreement about the processes called *attention, information processing,* and *memory*. These are not places in the brain, of course, but rather sets of interrelated processes that go on in the mind to facilitate the symbolic manipulation of information. This chapter is organized around these three processes.

....

Time Out

....

As you read this chapter, imagine that it is a presentation about how to listen to presentations. You want to learn enough from this chapter to be able to maximize your learning when you are participating in this way of learning. You want to remember enough of the main points to be able to get the most out of the presentation by the CEO next week.

....

ATTENTION
The Importance of Focus

When the gentle old Quaker was caught pounding his mule on the head with a stick, he defended his bellicose actions thus: "I'm not beating him, I'm just trying to get his attention." How often have teachers and parents told us to "pay attention?" It is good advice. The first problem you will have as you listen to an explanation is to discover what is important. Why should you want to pay attention to the general topic in the first place, and what are the parts of the presentation that deserve your special attention? What do people do when they pay attention to something?

A few key research studies provide the answer to those questions. Some of the earliest experiments on attention were designed to examine what happens when people try to listen to more than one thing at a time (Cherry, 1957).[4] Researchers asked subjects to listen to two separate but comparable messages through earphones, one message in one ear, another message in the other ear. In these experiments the subjects were directed to shadow (repeat after aloud) the message they were hearing in the designated ear. It is not surprising that subjects usually could report in great detail afterward what they heard in the designated ear, but when asked what they heard in the unattended ear, they floundered. Sometimes they could not even tell if the message had been changed to another language or played backwards. In other words, their attention was relatively undivided.

From these experiments researchers began to speculate that attention is like a *switch*—it is either on or off (Broadbent, 1958).[5] In subsequent experiments, however, other researchers discovered that subjects could process some things in the unattended ear (such as their own name), and these researchers decided that it would be better to think of attention as being more like a *filter* than a switch (Lindsey and Norman, 1972[6]; Triesman, 1960[7]). In general, however, they agreed that attention is highly focused.

Other experiments on attention explored the amount of attention required and available for different kinds of activities. Some activities simply require more attention than others and when that is the case, more mental energy is needed for paying attention. Capacity for paying attention, though limited, is not fixed; it varies with the difficulty of and familiarity with the activity. When sufficiently practiced, some activities are almost *automatic* and take very little attention while others are *deliberate* and require considerable attention (Shiffran and Schneider, 1977).[8]

What conclusions can be drawn from this research? The bad news is that our capacity for attention is perhaps more limited than we realize. The good news is that when it is necessary to attend closely to something, we have a rather remarkable ability to focus on what we want to see or hear while filtering out the rest.

Here are five rules that grow out of the research on attention.

Rule 1: *Pay attention.* Whatever it takes to force yourself to be interested in the topic, summon up the resources to do so. Ask yourself why it is important to be interested and why you must have this information.

Rule 2: *Focus.* You cannot pay attention to everything, so try to figure out what are the three main points, the five important ideas, the essence of the model, or the key to the process being presented. Try to distinguish between the trivial and the important, and focus on the most important things.

Rule 3: *Don't overload the system.* Because we all have a limited capacity for attention, focus on one thing at a time. Don't try to copy down the information from the overheads, listen to the lecturer, and glance through a report at the same time. Listen to the lecturer and use the overheads as a guide to what is important. Take notes on the main points.

Rule 4: *Refocus your attention periodically.* The harder the material, the more likely the mind will wander. Bring yourself back to attention and refocus on what is most important. We all have a limited attention span. Monitor it.

Rule 5: *Avoid distractions.* If someone comes in late to a lecture or enters your viewing or reading space, be aware that this can cause you to lose focus. Shut out distractions as much as possible, but if you cannot do this, realize that you lost your attention and you need to go back to the place where you lost it and start again.

Time Out

Did you notice how we tried to capture your attention with the old story about the Quaker and the mule? Then we posed a question and suggested that selected research studies would help you to answer that question. We summarized with a main conclusion and provided five rules. Can you summarize the main ideas about attention? Are you ready for the next section and the second main point?

INFORMATION PROCESSING
Making Meaning

Perceptions are *interpretations*. A traditional, commonsense view of perception is that a person simply sees or hears what is out there. The research done by cognitive psychologists challenges that view.

There is no one-to-one correspondence between what is out there and one's perception of it; rather, perceptions involve a highly complex mental interpretation of the main features of the sounds, words, sentences, and images presented to us. We are like electronic scanners (Sanford, 1985).[9] In developing the technology for scanning, now widely used to read zip codes and bank checks, computer scientists designed programs that would read letters and numbers. A process known as *template matching* was first developed to search for a predetermined shape. This works well for fixed patterns, but when a scanner must read a variety of shapes, such as those presented in many different type styles, or even handwriting, the problem becomes more complex. For example, what does a scanner have to do when it is asked which of the following figures are A's:

$$A \triangle V A {\scriptstyle a} F a$$

In this situation the electronic device does not have a template, but rather a bank of features associated with A's. The scanner knows that A's have some of these typical features:

$$/ , {\scriptstyle \wedge} {\scriptstyle \sigma} {\scriptstyle \neg} {\scriptstyle \Gamma}$$

It looks for these features and is programmed to "decide" whether the letter has enough characteristics to be called an *A*. A similar process is at work for us. Humans have a highly complex, feature-based pattern recognition system. As we process information we engage in a systematic effort called *feature analysis*. Psychologists call this *bottom-up processing*. This is the first part of what we do as we process information: we make interpretations of incoming stimuli.

Simultaneously, we are engaged in *top-down processing* which involves our efforts to *understand* what we are seeing and hearing (Zimbardo, 1985).[10] The top-down part of the theory emphasizes what the individual brings to the information in order to understand it. Researchers have found that *context, meaning,* and *prior knowledge* deeply affect our understanding of information.

We process things in the *context* of their surroundings; we look for the big picture and its frame. For example, in the diagram below, like elements tend to be grouped together so that we see rows of x's and rows of o's.

x x x x
o o o o
x x x x
o o o o

They could be arranged differently, couldn't they, so that columns dominate.

We also look for semantic *meaning*. For example, in processing the word *ice* in the sentence, "The car slid on the ice," a great deal of help is provided by the early part of the sentence, "The car slid on the. . . . " Naturally, we think of ice, not a banana peel. When we read we are not only examining letters and words, we are looking for meaning. In fact, it is not always necessary to have all the letters present to get the meaning:

> *Thix example xhould proxe xhe poixt.*

When we read, we process words, groups of words, and phrases—chunks of information—not individual letters. Consider the point by counting the number of F's in the following passage:

> *Finished files are the result of years of scientific study combined with the experience of many years.*

A count of less than six requires more careful reading. Why do we miss some letters? Because we read groups of words and look for meaning.

Meaning does not come out of thin air; it comes from *prior knowledge*. What a person already knows about the information being presented has a great effect on the speed and ease of processing it. If the presenter throws in an acronym that is foreign to you, you will have trouble processing it. But if you already know that GDP means gross domestic product and DOD means

Department of Defense, then you can use that prior knowledge to make sense of things. We not only have prior knowledge of words and terms; we also have prior knowledge of ideas, concepts and processes. There is considerable evidence that we organize this prior knowledge into *scripts, frames,* and *schemas,* and that we call up this prior knowledge rapidly and in pre-organized packets to make meaning of new information.

Processing information demands more than a passive response from the participants. To "get it" you need to be actively involved, fully engaged in trying to interpret and understand the information being presented. You can understand impressive amounts of new information if you look for context and meaning and use your prior knowledge.

Time Out

It might appear as you read this section that you are encountering a lot of ideas, new terms, and illustrations. To process the information here, you may wish to make an outline. The main ideas are quite simple and limited in number: Information processing consists of *interpretation* and *understanding*. Understanding involves *context, meaning,* and *previous knowledge*. As a participant, your role is to find the main ideas and organize the rest of the information around those main points.

Here are five more rules (continuous numbering) growing out of the research on information processing.

Rule 6: *Interpretation is natural.* You are not trying so much to absorb information as to develop and refine your perception of it. You are neither a sponge nor a camera. You are more like a scanner.

Rule 7: *Look for overall patterns.* Look for the forest, then look for the trees. Details take on importance when you perceive their place in the big picture.

Rule 8: *Look for context.* Where does this information fit? Where did it come from? How is it related to similar or different information? How can you use it?

Rule 9: *Search for meaning.* Try to make sense of the information. What key words or phrases carry the meaning? If you don't understand the meaning, ask for further explanation. Information alone is meaningless until someone makes sense of it.

Rule 10: *Build bridges from your prior knowledge.* Ask yourself what you already know about this topic. What packets of knowledge can you call on to make sense of the new information? What connections or comparisons can you make? If you lack the prior knowledge needed to understand the new information, ask for it or go get it.

Time Out

What will you do during the CEO's presentation? What is your role? Would it help to take notes? If so, what should you put in your notes? What should you do about the details and illustrations? Is there anything you could do to get ready for the presentation, such as reading last year's annual report?

MEMORY

Using Mnemonic Devices

If a presentation is more than a ritual or performance, then you will also want to remember the information. How do you remember things, and is it possible to improve your memory, or at least the way you use it?

After many years of research, cognitive psychologists have agreed on a distinction between short-term memory (STM) and long-term memory (LTM). They use these words in a technical way (Sanford, 1985).[11]

Short-term memory, sometimes called *working memory,* does not last very long or hold very much. It is used to keep information in mind long enough to decide what to do with it. STM is like a small video monitor that plays sounds and images constantly in your head. Long-term memory is what most people mean by memory, the capacity to remember information over time. It is more like your hard drive. LTM picks up where STM leaves off—after a few seconds—and goes on for weeks, months, and years.

Short-term memory is what we use to keep an unfamiliar phone number in mind long enough to dial the call. Research shows that we can only hold about seven bits of information, give or take two, in our heads before we start to get confused and forget. (Interestingly, there are seven digits in a local phone number.) If we wish to do something with the information in short-term memory, we need to convert it in some way so that we can save it in long-term memory. This conversion process is the key to remembering information.

Research has shown that most people think their memory records everything perfectly, like a human camcorder, but the trouble comes in playback. Research has also shown that this perception is false; the real problem is in recording and storage as well as playback (Loftus, 1980).[12] Memory works more like a computer than a videotape. Information needs to be entered systematically, and filed in a special place. The human computer, with its potentially huge and complex storage and retrieval system, relies heavily on the association of meaning conveyed by language. These associations are established through memory devices.

Here are some memory devices you should get in the habit of using:

- *Rehearsal.* This is the most frequently used and least effective memory device, but it has at least limited use (Sanford, 1985).[13] Rehearsal, sometimes called *rote learning,* involves repeating information over and over again (out loud or to oneself) until it "sinks in."

- *Encoding.* Encoding involves associating a key word with the word or words to be remembered. Using a synonym is one form of encoding, so is placing the new word in a memorable sentence. More complex encoding involves developing acronyms—HOMES to remember the Great Lakes (Huron, Ontario, Michigan, Erie, Superior)—or catchy sentences, such as "Every good boy does fine" to remember the lines on the treble clef in music notation (E,G,B,D,F). "Chunking" is another form of encoding—subdividing long strings of information into smaller chunks. It is easier to remember 100, 101, 110 than to remember 100101110. Oddly enough, elaborate and distinctive devices work best (Shepherd, 1967).[14]

- *Imagery.* Research shows that people generally find it easier to remember pictures than words and that vivid, bizarre, images work wonders. If you need to remember "airplane," "tree," and "envelope," picture an airplane with trees growing from the wings and envelopes hanging from the trees like leaves (Lorayne and Lucas, 1974).[15]

- *Place method.* This device involves mentally placing the to-be-remembered items in a spatial location. A grocery list might be remembered by placing each item on the list mentally at a different location in the kitchen: the milk in the refrigerator, the paper towels on their rack, a can of soup at the stove, and so forth (Loftus, 1980).[16]

- *Meaning making.* Information that has meaning is remembered more easily than nonsense. When you read a passage or listen to a presentation, look for the underlying meaning. Try to remember the message of the words and not necessarily the words themselves (Pompi and Lachman, 1967).[17] If you can put the message in your own words you are more likely to remember it.

Most so-called forgetting is the result of not using appropriate devices to remember. You really must put your mental cursor on SAVE and click. Don't expect to remember new information just because you read it or heard it. You need to save it. Here are five more rules (continuous numbering) growing out of the research on memory.

Rule 11: *Make short-term memory work for you.* Project the words and images on your own private STM screen and ask what is next. What do you need to do with the information coming your way?

Rule 12: *Give up the myth of automatic memory/faulty recall.* Realize that remembering is hard work, and become actively involved in trying to remember.

Rule 13: *Use memory devices.* Information needs to be transformed into something memorable and unforgettable. Use whatever techniques work best for you to assist the storage process. No storage, no retrieval.

Rule 14: *Get beyond rehearsal.* Saying the information over and over takes a lot of your time and does not work as well as other techniques.

Rule 15: *Create dramatic and bizarre devices because they work best.* Develop vivid images and odd associations, and you probably won't forget them.

Time Out

You realize that as you listen to the CEO's presentation you will need to make some choices about important things you want to remember, such as main ideas, certain facts and figures, or a key illustration, and you are enthusiastic about trying out these memory devices. Uh, oh! Did you forget them? Try to use an image (icon) for each one: for *rehearsal* picture a stick figure conductor with his orchestra in rehearsal; for *encoding* picture some Morse code, such as ● ● ● - - -; for *imagery* picture a tiny little camera; for *place method* picture an X for "x" marks the spot; and for *meaning making* use that famous brand name for candies called _____. Got it?

The guidance provided here for listening to (and watching) live presentations also applies to presentations of information in other forms. Naturally the guidelines work best when the presenter or author of materials is aware of and follows these same principles for communicating information. Unfortunately, this is not always the case.

Time Out

You have been talking to your friend Heather about what you have learned about listening to presentations. She is skeptical. "I've heard this guy before and he's very disorganized. He loads us up with facts and figures and he's very boring." You reply, "Well, Heather, he probably didn't get to be CEO through his speech-making talent." What do you need to do if Heather is right?

If you are in a situation where the presentation is not exactly user friendly, you may need to work twice as hard to attend to, process, and remember the main message. If the presentation does not begin with something that grabs and focuses your attention, you need to ask yourself where the speaker is likely to be going, what you should focus on, and why you should be interested. Look for the title, the real beginning of the presentation (after the introductions), and try to summon up interest. As you try to interpret and understand the message, look for clues, such as *first, second, third,* or *my first main point is.* If there is no explicit structure, impose your own structure and three main points, two subpoints, and so forth. Develop an outline and try to fit details into the outline, even if they aren't presented in an orderly way. You will be lucky if the presenter assists you with remembering important ideas, but more likely you will need to use the memory devices as you go along, inventing clever images or codes, or extracting and filing away your own meaning of the main message in your own words.

Keep in mind that with all presentations, even those that are poorly organized and delivered, your goal is to maximize your learning. Your need for learning is so great in this new era that you cannot afford anything less. If the presentation is excellent, you have an opportunity to learn even more by applying what you know about cognitive learning.

LESSONS LEARNED

Ten Things You Can Do to Maximize Your Learning

1. Pay attention and refocus your attention as necessary.

2. Focus on main ideas and decide what is important.

3. Don't overload the system by trying to attend to too much at once.

4. Look for features and patterns in the information being presented and find a structure or invent an outline.

5. Search for context and meaning.

6. Build bridges to your prior knowledge.

7. Make short-term memory work for you while you jot down notes and reactions.

8. Use memory devices and make active efforts to remember what you think is important.

9. Apply the rules to your responses to written presentations as well.

10. Maximize your learning even when the presentation is poor, and get the most from effective presenters.

The Third Way of Learning

LEARNING TO THINK

. . . .

Inquiry Learning

THE FAMOUS FRENCH SCULPTOR RODIN idealized thinking in his bigger-than-life, chin-on-fist rendering of *The Thinker*. Our everyday language is full of references to thinking. We say "I need more time to think." "Let me think that over." "She is good at thinking on her feet." What is thinking? Is asking questions a way of learning?

In this new era, overwhelmed as we often are by the sheer amount of information at our disposal, we often wonder if the information we have is any good. In addition to acquiring information, we need to evaluate it and decide what to do with it. If the second way of learning is about processing and remembering information, the third way of learning is about criticizing information, transforming it, and using it. This is done by asking a lot of questions, and the learning process is commonly referred to as *inquiry*.

Richard Paul, a major leader in the international critical thinking movement, describes the nature of the work that is increasingly required in the workplace as *intellectual work* (1995, 113).[1] Intellectual work requires thinking. Effective thinkers in the workplace are the people who generate ideas, develop and ana-

83

lyze proposals, invent new products, devise new services, suggest quality improvements, or sift through the information flowing through the organization to distinguish sense from nonsense.

Time Out

Imagine that you have been asked by your company to join a task force to suggest new product lines. The task force, which cuts across established divisions in its composition, is one of five being established as part of a company initiative to improve employee thinking skills and enhance organizational learning. This is the second year for the program. You will receive training to develop thinking skills, but the assignment is real. Last year, one of the task force ideas for new products was selected by top management and approved by the board for development and implementation. You are enthusiastic about the training and you are wondering how to get the most out of this opportunity for learning.

Because it is customary to define learning as *remembering facts,* we sometimes forget that asking questions is actually a way of learning. In fact thinking, as a systematic way of asking the right questions, may be the oldest way of learning.

Unlike cognitive psychology, with its rather recent origins, efforts to understand thinking have their roots in classical antiquity. Philosophy, as a way of thinking about thinking, preceded science by more than two thousand years, and many of the guidelines used by effective thinkers today go back to Plato and Aristotle. Modern efforts to define and measure critical thinking were initiated by Edward Glaser (1941),[2] and much of our understanding of creative thinking relies on the more recent theories of J.P. Guilford (1986)[3] and E. Paul Torrence (1995)[4].

LEARNING THROUGH INQUIRY
Thinking About Thinking

What is thinking and why is inquiry a way of learning? The random thoughts that pass through our heads as we shower or drive along the highway are called *nondirected thinking,* which is different from purposeful *directed thinking* (Halpern, 1984).[5] Directed thinking includes asking questions, analyzing and making arguments, identifying reasons, formulating hypotheses, seeking and weighing evidence, distinguishing facts from opinions, judging the credibility of sources, classifying data, making definitions, using analogies, making value judgments, and generating creative ideas. Directed thinking also involves certain habits of mind, such as being well informed and open minded, considering opposing viewpoints, respecting evidence, suspending judgment, tolerating ambiguity, being curious and skeptical, and revering the truth (Ennis, 1987).[6]

Three types of thinking are especially important in organizational settings: critical thinking, creative thinking, and dialogical thinking.

- *Critical thinking* has been defined as "judging the authenticity, worth, or accuracy of something, such as a piece of information, a claim or assertion, or sources of data" (Beyer, 1985, 19).[7] Critical thinking focuses on the set of *reasons* set forth as the *justification* for an *argument* (Kurfiss, 1988, 2).[8]

- *Creative thinking* is "thinking guided—indeed driven—by a desire to seek the original. It involves mobility; it revels in exploration; it requires flexibility; it honors diversity" (Beyer, 1985, 33).[9] Instead of following rules, creative thinkers break them. Creative thinking usually results in creative products or services, inventions, or new processes.

- *Dialogical thinking* involves being able to evaluate different points of view and frames of reference and to see both sides of an argument (Paul, 1987, 128).[10] Through dialogical thinking—a kind of role playing of another person's thinking—we are able to enter opposing arguments and viewpoints, thereby examining the strengths and weaknesses of our own thinking.

Learning through inquiry is a way of learning that proceeds by asking questions. You may have encountered it in school settings under the vague name of "discussion" or experienced it in science labs. It sounds easy enough—just asking questions—but it is the type, content, and sequencing of questions that are important. There is an art of inquiry, and it is learned best by actually engaging in asking questions under expert guidance. Usually this is done in groups, but sometimes it is practiced under individual supervision. Above all, practice is important. You learn inquiry by actually asking questions.

Time Out

Have you ever noticed how some people are really good at asking questions? They sit in a meeting, listening, without much to say, but then just at the right time they jump in and ask a very intelligent question. Heads turn, the room grows silent. Sometimes an entire proposal falls apart over one simple little question. How do they do that?

Some people say that it is impossible to improve one's thinking skills because thinking is mainly a matter of intelligence. Evidence is mounting, however, for the view that intelligence and thinking ability are not the same thing (Nickerson, et. al., 1985).[11] "Intelligence relates more to the raw power of one's mental equipment. Raw power of intelligence is one thing, the skilled use of it is something else" (44).[12] Researchers have come to see that thinking involves other important elements besides intelligence, including *knowledge* (the subject one is thinking about), *operations* (the steps and processes used), and *dispositions* (atti-

tudes or habits of mind about thinking). All can be improved
through learning (Beyer, 1985, 20, 25).[13]

To master the art of inquiry as a way of learning, the first step
is to learn more about critical, creative, and dialogical thinking,
so that you know what questions to ask and how to ask them.

Time Out

You go to the first training session for the five task groups, and spend
the first morning listening to a presentation on critical thinking. Okay,
you know how to listen to presentations. The facilitator promises
that you will have a chance that afternoon to practice what you have
learned. The following section is a summary of what was explained
to you on the first morning.

ASKING THE RIGHT QUESTIONS
Critical Thinking

We are challenged to do critical thinking when we encounter
written or spoken efforts to present a point of view, such as a
report, plan, proposal, or position paper. The point of view is
often buried in a lot of information and is sometimes disguised,
therefore, as "just the facts." You can learn to be a more effective critical thinker by examining any expressed point of view
for these key elements and by asking these questions:

- *Assertions. What assertion is being made?* An assertion is a
  statement that states positively something to be true (Nickerson, 1986, 35).[14] Look first for the assertions. What are they?
  What do you want to ask about them?

- *Opinions and Beliefs. Is this assertion an opinion or belief
  (20)?*[15] An example of an opinion is "Pepsi tastes better than

Coke." An opinion is a matter of taste. Nothing will settle this dispute. A belief, on the other hand, can be supported by evidence. If someone says, "More people in Ohio prefer Pepsi to Coke," it is possible to gather evidence (for example, through a consumer survey) to support the belief. Ask yourself: What kinds of assertions are you examining?

- *Warranted Beliefs. Can the belief be supported?* Warranted beliefs have evidence to back them up. A belief with a lot of evidence is sometimes called a *factual statement* (Schwarze and Lape, 1997, 49–50).[16] When the belief corresponds to a state of affairs and there is good evidence for it, we are more likely to believe it. That is why it is called a belief. Ask yourself: What is the evidence?

- *Arguments. What is the argument?* An argument is not just a verbal disagreement. In a technical sense, arguments are statements (assertions) constructed so as to support a conclusion (Nickerson, 1986, 68).[17] The purpose of an argument is to convince. Ask yourself: What argument is being built here, to convince me of what?

- *Conclusions. What is the conclusion?* The first part of an argument to look for is in fact the last part, the conclusion. Conclusions are the part of the argument that the maker of the argument wants you to believe. *Descriptive conclusions* are statements about a present situation. *Prescriptive conclusions* are statements about what ought to be done (Browne and Keeley, 1994, 16).[18] Reasonable people often disagree about the current state of affairs and what ought to be done about it.

- *Premises. What are the premises of this argument?* Premises are the statements that provide evidence, the facts and figures to support the conclusion (Nickerson, 1986, 36).[19] Premises are also debatable because they aren't just facts, they are arrangements of evidence. Sometimes the "facts" are not really true, and other important facts may have been ignored.

- *Assumptions. What are the assumptions behind the argument?* Assumptions are statements that people already believe and are obvious, or they are statements that no one has questioned (Nickerson, 1986, 36).[20] Assumptions are dangerous because they are often used as evidence and often go unchallenged or unidentified. Look for unexamined assumptions.

As you become more skilled at finding the argument, you will notice four kinds:

- *Inductive arguments* are bottom-up arguments built systematically from evidence. If you bite into a green apple and it is sour, you form a hypothesis: Maybe green apples are sour. If you check out a lot of green apples and they are all sour you are ready to draw a conclusion: Green apples are sour (Corbett, 1991, 11–46).[21] Most scientific research uses inductive arguments.

- *Deductive arguments* are top down arguments that have an inner logic. They begin with what looks like a conclusion: All hard green apples are sour. You are offering me a hard green apple, therefore, it must be sour. The new conclusion has been reasoned out from the premise; it is a logical conclusion.

- *Legal arguments* are the kind used in courtrooms. There is a claim (my client is innocent) and a lot of disputed evidence. A claim is not absolute, so it can be established or rebutted, but in legal arguments we usually find degrees of proof, not certainty. That is why juries disagree. In these arguments you look for *argued probabilities* (Corbett, 1991, 42–45).[22]

- *Analogies* are comparisons, and arguments that use analogies draw their strength from the similarities of the things being compared. For example, the argument might be made that being a good manager is like being a good parent. The argument works to the extent that similarities exist, but the analogy breaks down (as all analogies do) when crucial differences are made clear (Corbett, 1991, 21–23).[23] Ask yourself: How well does this analogy hold up?

As you conduct your inquiry by using the skills of an effective critical thinker and looking for the kinds of arguments being used, you can also watch for key problem areas addressed by critical thinkers, such as the following:

- *Definitions.* Sometimes people who are putting forth or discussing a report or proposal have not used clear definitions. The participants are not talking about the same thing, although they may think they are. You can ask for clear working definitions for the purposes of discussion.

- *Language.* Language is used in different ways—sometimes precisely, sometimes metaphorically. It is important to know how language is being used, and for meanings to be as clear as possible. Note how meanings get confused when someone says:

  "He cooks carrots and peas (pees) in the same pot."

  Does he cook two vegetables, or does he cook one vegetable in a pot that he also uses for urination (Halpern, 1984, 27)?[24] You can look for confusion that grows out of ambiguous or imprecise use of language and point this out.

- *Categories.* Ideas often need to be put into larger bundles called categories. The sorting and classifying of ideas is often necessary to discover what goes with what. Categories are not always known in advance; sometimes they emerge from the discussion. You can help establish and name categories, and then get the particulars in the right places. This often involves making lists.

- *Relationships.* Clear thinkers note how one idea or category of ideas is related to another. Can the ideas be put into a matrix or web? Is the relationship among the ideas causal, spatial, temporal, linear, circular, or spiral? Because participants in an inquiry are often too close to the ideas to see the connections, you can ask about these relationships. Sometimes it helps to make drawings that chart the relationships of ideas.

One additional tool that will help you sharpen your critical thinking is the ability to identify *logical fallacies.* There are certain hazards to avoid in critical thinking, and for some reason, people who are perhaps too eager to present their point of view tend to repeat common mistakes again and again (Corbett,

1991[25]; Browne and Keeley, 1994[26]; Nickerson, 1986[27]). Some of these mistakes are:

- *Ad hominem argument*—attacking the person, not the idea; name-calling

- *Association*—attaching credit or discredit to an idea by associating it with a person or group

- *Appeals*—to authority, tradition, or numbers for support

- *Stereotyping*—using labels and "boxes" to avoid more careful examination

- *Glittering generalities*—employing sophisticated jargon or fancy phrases that cloud understanding

- *Equivocation*—changing the meaning of a term as the discussion proceeds

- *Begging the question*—restating the same conclusion rather than examining the argument (not to be confused with "calling into question")

- *Red herring*—changing the subject to alter the course of the discussion

- *False dilemma*—setting up only two alternatives when there may be more

- *Simple explanation*—failing to recognize or give credit to rival explanations

- *Selective use of evidence*—gathering and using only the evidence that supports a position while avoiding contrary evidence

- *Overgeneralization*—concluding too much from limited evidence

- *Hasty closure*—jumping to conclusions

- *Seeking the perfect solution*—rejecting partial solutions, when these may be the best available

Time Out

Armed with this new understanding you go into the afternoon session ready to practice what you learned. The facilitator passes out copies of a speech given by the chairman of the board five years ago. You never thought of a speech as an argument before, but the facilitator explains that the job of the participants is to think critically about the assertions, arguments, conclusions, assumptions, type of argument, problems, and logical fallacies in the speech.

The speech is five pages long, but in a nutshell, the chairman's argument is that this is a wholesale company. We do lumber, fishing, and mining, and we sell in bulk quantities. We don't manufacture and we don't retail because we don't know how. That is our mission.

Soon everyone is raising questions: Who says? Why is that? Why not? What is the evidence? What is the assumption behind that position? Everyone is thinking deeply, some for the first time, about the true potential of the company. The next morning is devoted to a presentation on creative thinking.

GETTING BRIGHT IDEAS
Creative Thinking

Creativity is a complex matter and not something that can be established in an ongoing way by participating in a few workshop activities. You can, however, learn about creative thinking and become better at it through sustained practice. The first step is to get a better grasp of what creativity is.

Some of the earliest studies of creativity stressed inherited genius (Weisberg, 1993).[28] Modern theories of creativity build on the work of J.P. Guilford (1986, 41–50),[29] who suggested that certain factors are associated consistently with creativity, and that to some extent these can be learned and developed. Guilford named and described these factors:

- *Sensitivity to problems*—ability to notice problems and opportunities for creativity

- *Fluency of ideas*—the number and complexity of ideas produced, particularly ideas that go off in new directions

- *Flexibility*—ability to alter one's mental set and make transformations of one thing into another

- *Originality*—uniqueness of response compared to the typical response of others

- *Redefinitions*—ability to redefine something and change its meaning

Guilford and his followers also added at a later time the idea of *elaboration*, the ability to work out the details of the original idea (Baer, 1993, 14).[30]

You can notice people who appear to exhibit behavior that matches these factors, and you can monitor your own thinking by asking yourself to look for creative opportunities, to let your creative ideas flow, to be more flexible and original, and to allow yourself to see things in new ways.

The creative process is often presented as a series of steps. Drawing on the work of others in the field, University of Chicago psychologist Mihaly Csikszentmihalyi (1996, 79–80)[31] suggests that the following steps can usually be observed:

- *Preparation*—becoming immersed in a set of problematic issues that are interesting and arouse curiosity

- *Incubation*—the "aha!" moment when the pieces of the puzzle fall together

- *Evaluation*—when the idea is examined further to see if it is worth pursuing

- *Elaboration*—working out the details

Csikszentmihalyi (1996)[32] strongly supports the idea that creativity needs to result in creative outcomes or products, followed eventually by public recognition of their value. He places considerable emphasis on becoming well grounded in a domain or field as a prerequisite to creative insights. His view supports the old adage, "Creativity favors the well-prepared mind," and he challenges the stereotype that creative people are weird or unbalanced, finding in his studies that they exhibit a combination of playfulness and discipline, the introvert and extrovert, the traditional and rebellious.

This understanding of creativity implies that to develop your powers of creative thinking, you will need to spend significant amounts of time on

- *Preparation*—becoming familiar enough with a field to be creative

- *Acquaintance*—learning about how the creative process works

- *Involvement*—working on concrete projects that stimulate and develop the creative process

....

Time Out

....

Having challenged the assumption about the exclusive wholesale mission of the company yesterday, the task groups begin to generate retail ideas for fish, lumber, and aluminum. At first the ideas are simple, such as smoking salmon, but soon people begin to combine ideas from different resource areas. You suggest the idea of smoked salmon wrapped in aluminum foil and marketed in pine boxes. Someone from marketing called Kristin sees great potential in that idea, but you realize it would take a lot of development. Soon

the room is full of other interesting ideas. You note that creative thinking involves having unusual ideas and asking the right questions
about them. Tomorrow's session is about dialogical thinking.

APPRECIATING ANOTHER POINT OF VIEW
Dialogical Thinking

Dialogical thinking involves "dialogue or extended exchange
between different points of view or frames of reference" so that
we can assess the strengths and weaknesses of our thinking and
experience the inner logic of alternative points of view (Paul,
1987, 292).[33]

Richard Paul (1987, 258)[34] suggests that human beings have a
tendency toward being *egocentric thinkers,* and that we all have
"a side of us willing to distort, falsify, twist, and misinterpret."
To overcome these egocentric tendencies in our thinking, we
need to work hard at becoming *fair-minded thinkers* (1987,
259–262).[35] At a minimum, this means being able to present sympathetically more than one side of an issue.

This sympathetic presentation can be achieved by role playing the thinking of another. What would those on the other side
of this issue say? How would they attack this argument? The
challenge is to become willing to enter sympathetically into
opposing points of view and thereby recognize the strengths
and weaknesses in one's own viewpoint. In such a discussion,
"people learn to experience the dialogical process as leading to
discovery, not victory" (Paul, 1987, 138).[36]

Dialogical thinkers learn to ask certain *root questions* that help
people get beyond the content of a particular set of ideas to a
deeper understanding of each other (Paul, 1987, 297).[37] You may
wish to use some of the following questions drawn from a longer
list developed by Richard Paul:

- How did you come to think this?
- Why do you believe this?
- What are some of the reasons why people believe this?
- Some people might object to your position by saying. . . . How would you answer them?
- What do you think of this contrasting view?
- What are the practical consequences of believing this?
- What would we have to do to put it in action?

Dialogical thinking enables you to loosen your emotional attachment to your own point of view. To practice dialogical thinking, try this technique: take the side that is losing the argument until it appears to be winning; then switch to the side that is losing and help them out. Become adept at stepping back and arguing both sides.

Time Out

In the afternoon the task groups select five of their most creative ideas from yesterday's discussion. The best case possible is made for developing that idea, but then the opposite case is built for not supporting that idea. You pair up with Kristen and try to explore the pros and cons of the idea for smoked salmon in a box. If the idea is selected for presentation to management, you will have anticipated most of the objections they will raise.

SEARCHING FOR ANSWERS
Framing Questions

Inquiry, as we have noted, is a way of learning that relies heavily on asking the right questions. But what are the right questions, and of all of the questions that could be asked, how should you go about selecting the right ones? Obviously, this takes experience, but as you can see from reading this chapter there is some theory and technique involved as well. You can learn to ask appropriate and incisive questions, the kind that move the inquiry toward better understanding and new insights.

If you find yourself in a structured situation, you can watch the facilitator to see what kinds of questions are being asked. Often this provides a good model for your own questions. Your role, of course, is to try to deal with the questions asked and use the exchange to sharpen your own thinking. As a participant, however, you also have the right and responsibility to ask questions. The kinds of questions you ask and the way you frame them will contribute greatly to the quality of the inquiry.

The art of asking questions has been explored in a useful book by J.T. Dillon (1990)[38] entitled *The Practice of Questioning*. Based on that work, we offer these guidelines.

- *Choose your questions carefully.* What will be learned through your question and how will it move the inquiry toward greater understanding?

- *Phrase questions carefully.* Questions will be answered differently depending on the words you use.

- *Anticipate answers.* Project likely answers and anticipate what you will do with them.

- *Use open questions.* Employ questions that make room for a wide range of responses and avoid questions that can be answered yes or no.

- *Avoid dichotomous questions.* Either/or questions do not foster inquiry. Ask questions that invite multiple alternatives.

- *Use narrative questions.* These questions invite a story rather than a verification, such as, "Tell me what happened when . . ." rather than, "Were you at home on Friday?"

Not all inquiry is done collectively. Sometimes you will be working alone, analyzing a particular report or proposal. But all of the guidelines, steps, and suggestions offered above still apply. Some people actually prefer to do their thinking alone and although some stimulation is sacrificed, the quality of outcome may increase with solitude. Remember, inquiry is actually a way of learning, and some of your best learning may occur when you are thinking things out on your own.

LESSONS LEARNED
Ten Things You Can Do to Maximize Your Learning

1. Acknowledge inquiry as a way of learning.

2. Realize that thinking skills can be learned and improved.

3. Look for assertions, conclusions, premises, and assumptions when you analyze arguments.

4. Watch for inductive, deductive, and legal arguments, and for arguments that use analogies.

5. Attend to definitions, precise use of language, categories of ideas, and relationships among ideas.

6. Identify and avoid logical fallacies.

7. Understand what creativity is and realize that it takes preparation.

8. Know and follow the stages of the creative process.

9. Try to understand both sides of an issue.

10. Learn to ask useful and appropriate questions.

LEARNING TO SOLVE PROBLEMS AND MAKE DECISIONS

· ·

Using Mental Models for Learning

HOW DO YOU REACT when someone gives you a problem? Try this one (Fixx, 1978)[1]:

If you have black socks and brown socks in your drawer—mixed in a ratio of four to five, how many socks will you have to take out to make sure of having a pair of the same color?

Are you eager for the challenge posed by a problem? Do you know how to approach problems? Does a chapter that begins like this make you want to turn to the next chapter?

Problems—big and small—are everywhere. In the workplace they arise from things that go wrong, but they are also embedded in opportunities. A problem is a question proposed for solution or discussion—usually a matter involving doubt, uncertainty, or difficulty. Most problem solving and decision making gets complicated. Usually several considerations enter the picture at once, and it becomes difficult to keep them straight. You can feel like a juggler trying to keep all the tenpins in the air, or a circus performer trying to spin a dozen plates at once. Such an act "boggles the mind," we say, and to boggle, the dictionary tells us, is to alarm, astound, shock, or stagger. So the mind must find some alternative to getting boggled. Psychologists call this boggling *cognitive overload*. The mind needs some system for dealing with the complexity posed by problem solving and decision making. This is why we turn to *mental models*.

....

Time Out

....

Did the problem about the socks boggle your mind at first? Does it make you a little anxious?

....

The first thing you can do, when the agenda calls for problem solving, is to maintain your composure and avoid panic. Frustrated by years of struggling with homework problems, and because there was no school subject called "problems in general," many people have come to hate problem solving. Without workable problem-solving strategies, we experience high levels of frustration. What we learn from this frustration is to avoid problems, what Brandsford and Stein (1993, 8–9)[2] call the "let me out of here approach" to problem solving. The first step is to persist.

AVOIDING A BOGGLED MIND
Understanding Mental Models

We use mental models all the time in our daily lives to develop simplified pictures of how things work—such as the human digestive process, the clutch on a car, or the orbiting of the planets around the sun. "The mental pictures we form of the component parts of these systems and how these parts interact are called mental models" (Ward, et. al., 1995, 53).[3] When we are asked, for example, which dogs have ears that stick up above the head, we don't go through a memorized list, such as shepherd-up and beagle-down; we recall a mental image of what the dog looks like (Glucksberg, 1988).[4]

Most expert problem solvers use mental models to proceed through the various steps involved in solving a problem. Decision makers use mental models to weigh the options in a decision and to predict likely outcomes.

The mental models theory has a fascinating history. Some of the early research on apes done by Wolfgang Koehler suggests that even lower animals have problem-solving abilities. When given boxes and sticks to arrange in order to be able to go after a banana at the top of their cage, apes appear to have moments of insight (Dworetzky, 1985, 237–38).[5] Were they using mental models? Modern research on problem solving proceeds from the work of Karl Dunker in 1945, who asked his subjects to think aloud as they attempted to solve problems so that he could track their techniques (Dellarosa, 1988).[6] The classic work on problem-solving theory is Allan Newell and Herbert Simon's *Human Problem Solving* (1972).[7] Decision-making theory has its roots in the philosophy of Blaise Pascal (1623–1662), who developed what has come to be regarded as the first decision analysis technique (Baron, 1994, 315).[8]

As with critical, creative, and dialogical thinking there is a growing awareness that the skills needed for problem solving and decision making can be learned. There are guidelines to follow and techniques to use. Practice in applying those guidelines and techniques usually comes through cases or projects that embody real world problems to be solved or decisions to be made. There are things you can do to maximize your learning in these settings.

Time Out

How are you doing with the problem about the socks? Would it help if you had a systematic way of approaching that problem and other problems you encounter?

ESTABLISHING A FRAMEWORK
A Basic Problem-Solving Model

Newell and Simon (1972, 53–63, 787–791)[9] provide the classic problem-solving model now found in most texts on the subject, the components of which are reviewed briefly here.

- *Goal state.* A problem calls for a solution. It is important to have some idea of the goal, some picture of what things will be like when the problem is solved. What are the criteria against which a solution will be judged? What is the problem statement calling on you to do or to determine?

- *Initial state.* The conditions and information provided up front can be considered the "initial state." What information do you have to work with when you start?

- *Problem space.* The gap between the goal state and initial state is the problem space, the bounded area where the problem can be worked out.

- *Solution paths.* These are the options generated as potential solutions to the problem. Solution paths are the ideas people generate to try to solve the problem.

- *Operations.* Certain mental activities often need to be performed to move from initial state to goal state. Mental models are often useful here because the operations can involve a flood of information and ideas.

- *Barriers.* The problem space presents certain barriers. It is not easy to move from initial state to goal state; if it were easy, there would not be a problem.

Newell and Simon's general framework for thinking about problems is in itself a useful mental model into which more specific models fit. Using this framework is an essential first step.

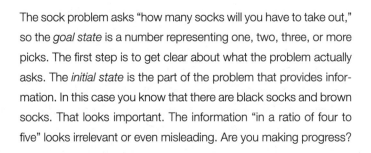

Time Out

The sock problem asks "how many socks will you have to take out," so the *goal state* is a number representing one, two, three, or more picks. The first step is to get clear about what the problem actually asks. The *initial state* is the part of the problem that provides information. In this case you know that there are black socks and brown socks. That looks important. The information "in a ratio of four to five" looks irrelevant or even misleading. Are you making progress?

GENERATING SOLUTIONS
Using Mental Models

What happens in the problem space is crucial, of course, and that is where mental models come into play directly. These are some of the mental models that can be used to attack problems directly.

Random search. This is sometimes called *trial and error.* Random search works when the number of options is small and every possible option can be examined directly. For example, in working with the anagram THA, there are only six possible solution paths for arranging the letters to make a word: THA, TAH, ATH, AHT, HTA, and HAT. The problem solver will arrive at HAT, eventually and inevitably, even if it is last, through trial and error. This model works in some situations, but if there are many potential solution paths and the paths themselves are complex, a better model is needed. Some would say that random search is not an intelligent approach to problem solving, and for that reason is not really a mental model (Halpern, 1984, 189).[10]

Hill climbing. Picture yourself blindfolded on a hill. Your goal is to get to the top. You start out in some direction and you get some feedback from your legs that this is downhill. You try again and start moving up. Your steps are small but you can see that you are getting closer to the goal. Physicians sometimes use the hill-climbing model to arrive at the right dose of medicine (Baron, 1994, 68).[11] With this model you say, "Let's try this and get some feedback; then let's try this."

Means-ends analysis. If the goal is the end, and the means of getting there is not clear, it is sometimes useful to find subgoals and then devise the means for reaching these. A frequently cited example is the Tower of Hanoi Problem shown in the figure below (Halpern, 1984, 182-4).[12]

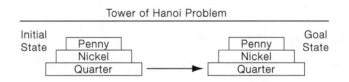

Tower of Hanoi Problem

The object is to move three coins of one stack (quarter, nickel, penny, with the quarter on the bottom) from the first site to the third site and restack them in the same order at the third site by using the intermediary site for staging and moving only one coin at a time. For this problem it is best to work in steps. One subgoal is to get the quarter to the third site. Another subgoal is to get the nickel and penny off the quarter so it can be moved. That can be done by moving the penny to the third site, the nickel to the second site, and the penny back to the nickel. This leaves the third site vacant so the quarter can be moved to it. And so forth. The mental operations for many problems can be managed in this way by breaking the problem into subgoals and then working on them one at a time, step by step.

Working backward. The natural question for all of us to ask is, "What should I do first?" With certain kinds of problems, it may be best to ask, "What should I do last?" Next to last? And so on, back to the beginning. The paper and pencil mazes that children enjoy can be more easily solved by starting at the goal and working backward (Halpern, 1984, 184–5).[13] Most event planning or project management works best by setting the final date and working backward through the supporting logistics.

Split-half method. You can guess the age of anyone under one hundred by asking the subject first if they are under fifty. If the answer is yes, the next question is whether the subject is over twenty five. The next question always splits the remaining amount in half until the answer is found. You will never need to ask more than seven questions to establish someone's age using this method (Halpern, 1984, 192–3).[14] Some problems can best be solved through a narrowing-down process.

Simplification. Some problems are so complicated, that it is useful to try to suspend the rules temporarily or cut out some of the details. (Wickelgren, 1974, 46–47).[15] Ask yourself, "What is the essence of this problem, the main goal, the central outcome?" Try to reduce the problem to its simplest elements.

Using actual data. Many problems are hard to deal with in the abstract, but they sometimes become more manageable when actual numbers or objects are used (Wickelgren, 1974, 26).[16] Problem solving often involves plugging in the numbers to see whether a proposed solution will or will not work.

Contradiction. One way to eliminate potential solution paths is to see if they are contradictory to the "givens" in the initial state, or incompatible with what might reasonably be expected in the goal state. In some cases an eyeball comparison or an estimate will generate the awareness, "It *couldn't* be that!" (Wickelgren, 1974, 109–10).[17]

Graphs and diagrams. Some problems tend to overwhelm us with information. Often it is necessary to put the data into a better semblance of order. This may mean transforming data provided in narrative form into written lists, charts, or diagrams (Halpern, 1984, 167–74).[18] If you get the feeling that this is not the kind of problem you can solve in your head, start putting the information on paper in a way that enables a useful analysis.

Analogy. Perhaps the problem is analogous to another. Two problems that appear quite unrelated may have similarities when compared. Something learned from one problem may be applicable to another (Holyoak and Nisbett, 1988, 82–3).[19] The challenge, of course, is to find and apply good analogies and to be able to see the connections.

Time Out

For the sock problem, try a combination of *random search* and *using actual data*. Start pulling out socks. The first one is brown. The second one is black. The third one is brown (or black). What do you conclude?

WATCHING FOR TROUBLE
Avoiding Pitfalls

There are certain common pitfalls associated with problem solving, things to watch out for and avoid because they can cause trouble.

Misunderstanding the problem. People tend to rush into generating solutions before clearly defining the goal state or carefully analyzing the information provided in the initial state. Good information gets ignored and irrelevant information is regarded as valuable. When people rush into generating solutions to the sock problem, strange things happen. They have trouble seeing that the goal is to get one pair of socks of the same color guaranteed with the fewest picks. They think they need two pairs, or that the goal is to get the owner to reorganize his sock drawer so this problem will not occur. They make up all sorts of worries (are the socks the same size?) and rules (do I have to put each sock back in after I have taken it out?). They want to know if they can look into or dump out the whole drawer, and then sheepishly recognize that if they can, it won't be a problem anymore. They tend to ignore the most important piece of information in the initial state (that there are only two colors) and they tend to focus on irrelevant and misleading information (that the ratio of one color to the other is four to five). The solution comes fairly quickly when the problem is clearly understood.

Unrecognized presuppositions. Sometimes we bring presuppositions to the problem that greatly limit the solutions we will consider. Notice in this example the narrowing effect of a presupposition (Sanford, 1985, 46)[20]:

> *A man and his son were away on a trip. They were driving down the motorway when they had a terrible accident. The man was killed outright but his son was alive, though badly injured. The son was rushed to the hospital and was to have an emergency operation. In entering the operating theater, the surgeon looked at the boy and said, "I can't do this operation. This boy is my son." How can this be?*

The boy can be the son if one sheds the presumption that a surgeon must be a male; the female surgeon could indeed be the boy's mother.

Functional fixedness. When objects and concepts are defined in a rigid way, it is sometimes difficult to think of using them in any other way. A screwdriver, we know, is for twisting in screws, and it is hard to think of using a screwdriver for anything else because that is what it is for. If we stop thinking of it as a "screw-driver" and call it a "gadget," that rethinking may open up many more possibilities for its use (Glucksberg, 1988, 225).[21] The same is true for abstract concepts such as "cost" or "profit" or even "learning."

FROM PROBLEM SOLVING TO DECISION MAKING
Another Model

As problems are solved and solutions are generated, someone must make decisions about whether the solutions are actually good solutions. As with problem solving, decision making can boggle the mind. It is important to follow a rational decision-making model and to evaluate regularly the results that the model is producing.

....

Time Out

....

Here is a case. You find yourself on a personnel selection committee. One of the top positions in the organization is vacant. A brief job post-ing placed in key publications results in over one hundred applicants. These applicants are screened to the top ten by the agency helping with the selection, but now the committee is faced with selecting— making a decision about—the top candidate. Everyone begins to talk about which candidates they like best. What would you do?

....

The classic mental model for decision making has ten key steps (Halpern, 1984, 1–5)[22]:

1. *Determine values.* Begin at the end of the model and work backward. Values, in this instance, are statements of what has worth or utility. What values will this decision address?

2. *Determine outcomes.* What outcomes will fulfill the values? Outcomes are the specific results the decision will produce. Most decisions involve several desirable outcomes that reflect more than one set of values.

3. *Weight the outcomes.* Even if several outcomes are possible, they may not all be equally desirable. Outcomes can be ranked or assigned numerical weights that reflect importance. The weighting process establishes the relative importance of outcomes.

4. *Generate options.* Options can be plans, scenarios, products, services, or personnel. Options often grow out of problem solving. Not all decisions have good options, but a large number of suitable options improves the likelihood of good results.

5. *Identify attributes of options.* Options have attributes. For example, in a personnel decision, the candidates (options) usually have differing strengths and weaknesses (attributes). Having certain attributes may compensate for lacking others. What attributes of the options are most desirable?

6. *Match attributes to outcomes.* In a rational decision the attributes of the options are matched to the weighted characteristics of the outcomes.

7. *Make a choice.* After considering how various options will produce desired outcomes, make a choice and frame the choice as a decision rule; that is, as a recommendation.

8. *Cast the choice as a probability and consider the consequences.* Because no one knows how a decision will turn out, recommendations are usually presented as predictions cast as probabilities. What chance does this decision have for success? What is your willingness to bet on it?

9. *Predict the likelihood of outcomes.* In most decision making, people think the work is done when they have identified options. The hardest work may come in predicting outcomes. What risk is involved in this decision? What could happen?

10. Align the steps. Check the alignment of values, outcomes, and attributes of options involved in the actual choices. Do all the pieces fit together?

The steps of the decision-making model form a circle. The process starts with values and it ends up with values. One phase leads to another, but eventually the decision comes down to this: Which options with what attributes are most likely to result in the desired outcomes and values?

As you apply the steps to the personnel case, you realize that the committee needs to ask first what values and outcomes would be fulfilled by hiring a particular kind of person. What do people value most in the work this person does? Because several outcomes may be identified—good management, efficient financial control, effective human relations—the outcomes may need to be weighted or ranked for importance. Once these criteria are established, the options—in this case the ten candidates—can be examined in terms of their attributes. The attributes can be matched to the weighted outcomes. And so forth.

MORE TROUBLE
More Pitfalls

Like problem solving, decision making has its pitfalls. Here are some to avoid.

Wishful thinking. Sometimes known as the *Pollyanna Principle,* wishful thinking is the tendency to overestimate the chances of being successful. Wishful thinkers tend to overvalue the attributes of particular options, exaggerate the way options will attain outcomes, and overproject the probability of positive results (Halpern, 1984, 221–22).[23]

Entrapment. Decisions exist within the context of other decisions, and one decision, especially a bad decision, can affect another. Sometimes previous decisions have turned out badly, and because the decision has already cost a great deal in time, money, and effort, the decision maker is trapped in that previous decision and may make still another bad decision to try to save the first (Halpern, 1984, 222ff).[24] The best way to avoid this pitfall is to view each decision separately and approach it on its own terms.

Trade-offs. Trade-offs occur when we are willing to give up one outcome for another or compensate one attribute with another. Trade-offs are sometimes necessary, but having made one compromise, there is a tendency to make others. Sometimes it is necessary to draw the line with regard to what will and won't be given up in a decision (Baron, 1994, 346–49).[25]

Gambler's Fallacy. In so-called wheel-of-fortune games, there is a tendency to say "Number seven hasn't come up lately, so it is about time for it." In a truly random situation, however, every number on the wheel has a chance of coming up on every spin because the wheel has no memory (Halpern, 1984, 123[26]; Baron, 1994, 229–30[27]). In workplace decisions, probable outcomes are not likely to be random, like spinning a wheel, but people may still think, "We're due," "It's our turn," or "We've had our share of bad luck." Irrational behavior quickly intrudes on the rational decision-making process.

Misinterpreting trends. Predictions of the outcomes of a decision will sometimes rest on trends. Trends are tricky because they can change as new factors come into play. Trends are sometimes part of larger or related trends. For example, there may be a trend for older women to buy more sneakers, but is that part of a trend toward more exercising in the population, part of a trend toward more informal dress, or are there simply more older women as a proportion of the total population? Decision makers need to be careful in their use of trend data (Halpern, 1984, 23ff).[28]

LIVING LABORATORIES
Cases and Projects

The key to using mental models for problem solving and decision making is practice. It helps to learn about the steps and to become aware of different mental models, but there is no better way to learn problem solving than by solving problems and no better way to learn decision making than to make decisions. Usually these opportunities are provided through cases or equivalent real-life projects.

The idea of using cases for educational purposes has its modern roots in the case method of Harvard's School of Business, begun in 1909 (Pigors and Pigors, 1987, 415).[29] Originally known as the *laboratory method* or *problem method,* the case method gives the learner a chance to "put themselves in the decision maker's or problem solver's shoes." Cases have been called "the corpse for the student to practice on" (Leenders and Irskine, 1973, 110).[30]

No doubt you have already worked with cases or projects, or perhaps you will seek out this kind of learning. As with the other ways of learning, there are things you can do to maximize your learning when the case method is being used:

- *Be able to identify several types of cases and know which types are being used* (Pigors and Pigors, 1987, 415–19).[31] *Traditional cases* are presented in a written format with extensive background and current information, and may unfold over time through stages. *Live cases* are presented by a person who represents an organization. This person has lived through the case and makes a live presentation about it. The presenter may return at a later date to guide further discussion. *Key incident cases* involve a brief live presentation that stimulates questions, the answers to which provide the essential factual basis for the case.

- *Read the case carefully or listen closely to the presenter.* Get an overall understanding of the case. If the case poses one or more problems, begin to analyze those problems in terms of goal state, initial state, and problem space. Use mental models in the problem space to keep from getting a boggled mind. If the case presents the need for one or more decisions, try to apply the rational decision-making model.

- *If the case involves discussion, listen for a while to the chatter.* Some participants are bound to jump in with all their biases, assumptions, and gut-level reactions. Others will have important insights. As you listen, try to sort out what you believe are the real problems and decision points, and listen for sense and nonsense in the discussion.

- *If there is a facilitator*—there probably will be one—*notice how the facilitator defines the goals of the case and the expectations for learning.* Listen carefully for summaries, hints, changes of direction, suggestions, and feedback. Notice how the facilitator tries to focus the group on what is most important. The facilitator usually won't try to provide solutions or recommendations, but will provide a setting where participants can do so. The facilitator is like an orchestra conductor who knows the composer and the score (Barnes, et. al., 1994, 46).[32] Your role is to find out what instrument you are playing and when to play it. Watch the conductor.

- *Get involved.* Read the case more than once. Listen carefully. Speak when you can contribute. Volunteer to write a thoughtful response or make an analytical presentation. The opportunity will give you practice in learning to solve problems and make decisions.

- *If everything appears to be turning into a muddle, raise some of the basic questions* such as: What is the problem here? What would it be like when this problem is solved? What is the goal? What are the givens? What are the values we are trying to address through the outcomes of this decision? Does this decision have any chance of success? What are the risks?

Time Out

If you are in formal learning situations where cases are used, remember that cases are usually employed for practicing problem solving and decision making. If you want to practice these skills on your own, get some help in locating relevant cases to work on alone. Cases are used in many different fields—law, business, medicine, psychotherapy, social work, education—but the purpose is usually the same: developing abilities to solve problems effectively and make appropriate decisions. As for the sock problem, three picks for sure will get you a pair of black or a pair of brown. Right?

LESSONS LEARNED

Ten Things You Can Do to Maximize Your Learning

1. Avoid the "let-me-out-of-here" approach.

2. Don't let problem solving and decision making boggle your mind.

3. Use mental models.

4. Look for the goal state, initial state, and problem spaces.

5. Use mental models in the problem space to generate solution paths.

6. Avoid the pitfalls of misunderstanding the problem, unrecognized assumptions, and functional fixedness.

7. To assist in making decisions, use the ten-step rational decision-making model.

8. Make recommendations that project outcomes as probabilities.

9. Avoid the pitfalls of wishful thinking, entrapment, trade-offs, Gambler's Fallacy, and misinterpretation of trends.

10. Know what kind of case is being used, what is expected of you, what the facilitator is doing, and what you can do to contribute.

The Fifth Way of Learning

LEARNING IN GROUPS
. . . .
Collaborative Learning

TWO HEADS ARE BETTER THAN ONE, so it is said. What about three, four or five heads? Most people who work in organizations have some experience with groups, from the simple weekly staff meeting to participation on high-performance teams. Many organizations now rely on some form of team collaboration to achieve their goals. Groups and teams are also used to facilitate learning; that is, for *educational* purposes.

. . . .

Time Out
. . . .

Imagine that you and your friends, Yuko and Richard, have enrolled in a workshop on group communication. Yuko grew up in Japan where it was considered rude even to ask a question of the teacher. She is very shy and worries about participating appropriately in the group activities. Richard, on the other hand, tends to be an over-participator and knows he is not a very good listener. You are wondering what kind of learning actually results from group activities.

. . . .

The self-conscious use of groups for educational and therapeutic purposes had its origins in *employment* settings in the
early work of Elton Mayo at Western Electric in the 1930s, in the
experience of Kurt Lewin and his associates in 1946 in the development of the basic skill training group (t-group), and in the
work of Carl Rogers after World War II in the development of
personal growth groups (Hare, 1976).[1] Since that time, a great
amount of research has been done on groups and there is general agreement on how groups work and what to expect from
them. Most of the theory has come from the field of human communication studies.

Time Out

On the first day of the workshop, the facilitator breaks the class into
several groups of five people each. You are handed a sheet of paper
with brief instructions to think about the following problem silently for
two minutes and then discuss it in your group.

*A man bought a horse for $60 and sold it for $70. Then he bought
it back again for $80 and sold it one more time for $90. How much
money did he make in the horse-trading business?*

Yuko is nervous that she won't have anything to say. George thinks
he knows the answer. You are wondering what can be learned from
such a silly exercise. After you work on the problem for fifteen minutes, the facilitator conducts a debriefing and then summarizes in a
brief explanation what can be learned in groups.

DIVERSE OUTCOMES
What You Can Learn in Groups

Research has shown that groups are especially good for diverse kinds of collaborative learning:

- *Generating ideas.* Groups produce more ideas (Lorge, 1958).[2] People pool their ideas in groups, but there is something about the interaction in a group that stimulates more ideas. Sit by yourself and think about the horse-trading problem and you will probably come up with two or three interesting ways to look at it. Take it to a group and you will probably hear a host of viewpoints you never considered. As the ideas are discussed with others, you find that all of you are now thinking up new ideas that no one had thought about before your interaction. No one has said that groups always produce good ideas; but they do produce a *lot* of ideas.

- *Communication and human relations.* Groups are designed for communication and are good for learning human relations or enhancing communication skills. People in groups talk or act, and there is always some message in the communication. Even in a brief discussion of the horse-trading problem, you would notice that some people communicate boldly while others hardly say anything; some have good ideas, others just like to talk; some are fluent speakers and others are good listeners. Groups are excellent vehicles for learning how to communicate, how to establish one's "voice," and how to speak and listen in ways that are productive and effective.

- *Changing attitudes.* Groups are a powerful vehicle for influencing attitudes, opinions, and beliefs (Berelson and Steiner, 1964).[3] Persuading people to change their beliefs through argument or propaganda is very difficult, but in a group where everyone is openly exploring feelings and ideas, real change is more likely to take place. Many people, after discussing the horse-trading problem in their group, will change their opinion about the right answer. Groups are used for helping people overcome fears, work through disturbing feelings, give up self-defeating habits, reconsider long-standing beliefs, clarify values, and develop more positive attitudes. Groups are valuable for examining matters of the heart.

• *Practicing teamwork.* Groups are valuable for learning about collaboration. People learn teamwork by actually working in teams. Even after a short time working on the horse-trading problem, group members will begin to function as a team. They soon discover whether they would be a good team to work on other projects or whether they would need to learn more about collaboration. Teamwork involves cooperation, communication, taking responsibility, developing cohesiveness, and setting aside personal needs to work toward a common goal. Teamwork produces outcomes that cannot be reached by individuals working alone (Larson and LaFasto, 1989).[4] Teamwork can be learned.

The first thing to ask when you find yourself in a group is: What kind of learning can come from this group? Groups are often metaphors for some larger concept, so it is important to keep asking: What's the point?

Time Out

Next the facilitator reorganizes the class into groups of seven participants. The groups have five minutes to work on the activity, at which time a whistle is blown and a designated member must leave each group and go to the next. The facilitator emphasizes that success with the activity requires that each group learn from the rotating messengers, who continue to move each time the whistle is blown. The outcome depends on good work within the groups and good communication among the groups. At the end of the activity there is a brief discussion and the facilitator summarizes some points about organizing groups.

GETTING ORGANIZED
The Arrangements for Learning in Groups

In *facilitator-led groups* the facilitator is usually a part of the group and sits within the group or participates in its activities. Other groups are *leaderless groups* in the sense that the facilitator may have composed and set in motion several groups, but clearly remains outside these groups, perhaps looking in on them from time to time but not playing a significant role in the communication taking place in the group. *Leaderless* is probably a misnomer because most groups left to themselves will produce a leader. All groups, therefore, need leaders—but some groups have a formally designated leader called a facilitator.

A facilitator has several jobs. One is to compose the group or groups. One important thing to watch for here is the size of the group. A group needs to be big enough to get the work done, but small enough so that everyone can participate. Sometimes you need to tell the facilitator, "Our group is too big." One clue you have about this is when you see the group automatically subdividing itself into smaller groups.

A facilitator working directly with the group will monitor the communication of the group, will listen to and reflect back to the group what it is saying, and will often guide the direction of the discussion. The leader may hand out some directions or a task for the group. With leaderless groups, the facilitator will compose the groups—usually several small groups of three to seven—and will provide each group with a task and instructions called an *instrument*. Your role, in either situation, is to make sure that you and other group members are clear about the task and the ground rules. Sometimes the task just requires speaking, but at other times it involves getting up and doing things, some activity.

Often additional conditions are set for groups. For example, leaderless groups may be set up to compete with each other for a real or virtual prize for being first to finish or best in performance. Sometimes groups are instructed to cooperate and must collaborate to help each other or construct some larger activity or outcome. Often groups must report back to the whole, and an observer or reporter needs to be appointed. Depending on the arrangements for your group, you may need to nominate a facilitator, timekeeper, messenger, observer, or reporter.

Time Out

Groups of five persons are now composed with different membership than the previous groups. This time the activity is a little harder. It involves a problem about black and white marbles in different arrangements in boxes. You notice how people begin to talk almost immediately, how they seem to jockey for position, and take on different functions. Some people are really intent on solving the problem. Again, there is discussion and then a summary by the facilitator.

BECOMING INVOLVED
Task and Process

People who have studied groups note that the communication in groups seems to operate at two levels simultaneously—task and process (Goldberg and Larson, 1975).[5] At one level, group members are communicating about the task to be completed, the job to be done, the challenge presented in the instructions. At another level, group members are dealing with the *process* or social needs of the group. When people participate in groups they bring with them their individual needs for recognition, identity, status, power, visibility, competition, cooperation, and inclusion. All of these factors can and do affect the climate of the group and the group process. To function well, groups need some of both types of communication—task and process.

It is natural, therefore, for group members to socialize—and usually this communication is more than chit-chat. It helps group members feel comfortable and to begin to like each other enough to work together. On the other hand, a group that gets too involved with the process sometimes needs to be reminded of the task.

FINDING YOUR NICHE
Taking a Role

As groups mature, even over a short period of time, they develop a *structure* (Barker, et al., 1987).[6] Members take their places and begin to serve particular functions. The group's structure is not always obvious, but it is there. Some people, because they have more to contribute to the assigned task, or because they have more initial status or a strong personality, take a more central place in the group's structure, while others end up on the periphery. The composition of the group, its size and its communication patterns, all help to determine the group's structure.

Within the group, individuals take on roles (Benne and Sheets, 1948).[7] Some of these roles relate to the task, such as the

- *Information seeker,* who asks for clarification of ideas, facts or evidence.

- *Information giver,* who offers facts or relates his or her own experience.

- *Recorder,* who writes down suggestions or takes minutes.

  Other roles relate to the process, such as the

- *Encourager,* who agrees with, praises, and accepts the ideas of others.

- *Harmonizer,* who resolves conflict, mediates differences, and reduces tension.

- *Gate keeper,* who encourages others to participate and be heard.

Some individuals play negative roles that hinder the group's process, such as the

- *Aggressor,* who attacks others or the group as a whole.
- *Dominator,* who monopolizes the group or uses it for personal needs.
- *Blocker,* who opposes the ideas of others unreasonably and refuses to cooperate.
- *Clown,* who disrupts the group through excessive humor and horseplay.

Participants need to find their niche in the group. To maximize your own learning, it is necessary to be clear about what role or set of roles you are trying to play. Ask yourself what you have to contribute and how you can do it best. This involves assessing your own traits and abilities and matching them to what the group needs.

Groups are formed in various ways, but they all develop structure over time. Just because a group is formed and you are included, does not mean that those assembled are yet a group. Groups go through "stages," described by four rhyming words (Tuckman, 1965)[8]:

- *Forming*—a stage of testing and member independence, with emphasis on defining the task
- *Storming*—a stage of intragroup conflict and emotional expression
- *Norming*—a stage of development of group cohesion and establishing roles and rules
- *Performing*—a stage of effective functioning and the emergence of solutions

Note that if you enter a group late, many roles and norms will have already been established. Your entrance will be somewhat disruptive, so you need to catch up quickly, listen closely, and discover your niche. The same will be true when others enter a well-established group where you are a continuing member. You can help orient them quickly. Eventually—when members have found their niche, when rules have been developed, and when a certain amount of cohesion has been established—the group will begin to function well. You can watch for these things and help make them happen. If the group doesn't develop a structure and isn't functioning well, you won't learn much nor will anyone else.

Time Out

At lunch on the first day you compare experiences with Yuko and Richard. Yuko is greatly relieved to know that she has been able to participate effectively, primarily by finding her niche as recorder. You are impressed that so many kinds of learning can take place in groups. Richard is shocked to discover how dominating he has been, and he is excited about learning more about active listening in the afternoon session. You all agree that you began to like the people in your groups and that you were beginning to work together more effectively.

COMMUNICATION IN GROUPS
Sharing and Listening

Put people in groups and they will talk. Who talks and what do they talk about? How often do they talk? To whom do they talk? Who interrupts? Who listens? How do we know they are listening?

When one person interacts with another in a group, a communication event takes place that involves self-disclosure and feedback (Fisher, 1980).[9] *Self-disclosure* occurs when a person lets someone know something about themselves that the listener wouldn't ordinarily know. This can refer to any idea or feeling the person is expressing. The second part of this event occurs when someone else in the group, or several members, respond to what was said. People can respond in several ways by

- ignoring what was said.
- making another unrelated disclosure.
- making a disclosure that builds on the previous disclosure.
- responding to the disclosure by showing it was heard.

The first two responses don't do much for the communication process or the group. The third response helps, but the last is best: it provides *feedback*. Effective feedback involves active listening.

Time Out

For the first activity of the afternoon, participants are placed in pairs (dyads) and are instructed to share with each other their response to the statement "Are you more like a waterfall or placid lake?" Participants are urged to listen carefully while the other person is talking and then show that they are listening. After the activity, the facilitator summarizes.

Active listening has two parts, the listening part and the expressing part, and the expressing needs to be done in a way that demonstrates that listening occurred. The listener can pay attention to the ideas and content of what is being said, standing ready to agree or disagree, criticize, summarize, or conclude; or the listener can focus on feelings, trying to empathize with the speaker's emotions or viewpoint (Kelley, 1970).[10] Obviously, active listening encompasses both. Good listening involves avoiding interruptions, looking beyond the words to the meaning, and resisting the temptation to prepare an answer when you should be listening. The key to active listening, however, is in the feedback. Feedback is provided by

- summarizing key ideas briefly and checking to see if that is what was said.

- providing an interpretation of the meaning of what was said.

- labeling, discussing, or asking about the feelings behind what was said.

- comparing what was said to other things that have been said in the group.

- asking for elaboration or further explanation.

These are all things that an effective facilitator should model in providing feedback to group members, but groups need many active listeners and shouldn't rely on the facilitator to do all the listening. As a member of a group you need to take your turn in expressing yourself, of course, but you can make a significant contribution by becoming an active listener and providing clear and focused feedback to others.

Time Out

For the next activity the participants go outdoors, where they find a large orange plastic barrel full of little holes. A hose will start to fill the barrel with water. Group members can plug the holes by placing their fingers over the holes. The goal is to be able to fill the barrel to the top. There is just one rule. No one can speak; all communication within the group must be nonverbal. This activity opens up an interesting discussion of nonverbal communication, which the facilitator summarizes and expands upon.

Not all communication in groups is verbal. To be an effective participant you need to watch the nonverbal communication of others and monitor it in yourself. Sophisticated group watchers look for the following (Baird and Weinberg, 1970)[11]:

- *Proxemics*—the way group members arrange themselves in space through seating arrangements, physical distance, and general body orientation

- *Appearance*—overall physical appearance, dress, attractiveness, styles, or mood

- *Kinesics*—body movement, posture, gestures, and movement of the hands, limbs, and feet

- *Facial expressions*—facial features, movements of the eyes and mouth

Sometimes nonverbal communication reinforces or elaborates a spoken message, for example by using a gesture to accent an important point. At other times, however, a nonverbal message may contradict a verbal message, for example an arms-folded, tense denial of anger, which sends a visible clue to the group that what is being said is not what is being felt. In some group activities, the nonverbal message is the only communication. Keep in mind that in a sense, group members are always communicating whether they speak or not, through gestures, facial expressions, or the physical place taken in relation to the group. It is not possible to not communicate, because people are always sending messages and interpreting meanings, whether they are responding verbally or nonverbally, or doing nothing. If you withdraw and don't participate, that's also a message. The nonverbal messages sent by group members deserve appropriate feedback.

Time Out

At this point in the afternoon the workshop participants, in spite of being a little wet, are energized and full of questions. They have all been in groups at one time or another that did not work, and they start sharing their bad experiences with the facilitator, who is not surprised. He urges them to deal with the problems in groups and not leave everything to the facilitator. The following is some of what he said.

KEEPING ON TRACK
Overcoming Problems in Groups

Groups sometimes develop problems. You can be alert and watch for these problems and you can take action to keep these problems from interfering with your learning.

- *Conflict.* Some disagreement in groups is normal or even necessary, but excessive tension or open conflict can pull a group apart. When participants become impatient, stop listening, take sides, or make vehement attacks on each other, the facilitator will often step in (Bradford, et. al., 1970).[12] If there is no facilitator, as in so-called leaderless groups, the participants themselves must face and deal with the conflict. Sometimes conflict arises because of structural problems: the group doesn't have enough time or resources, or the group lacks a clearly defined task. If the conflict grows out of personality clashes or differences of opinion, standard procedures for resolving conflict—voting, compromising, finding common ground, addressing the issues—will probably work. The important thing—and here is where you can help—is that conflict must be faced and resolved. If everyone is ignoring a conflict, you can play a key role by identifying it and suggesting solutions.

- *Apathy.* The only thing worse than conflict is apathy—when participants don't care enough about the group to get involved.

When the conversation drags, when people wander away or come late, or when the level of participation is low or lacking energy, the group has a problem. Apathetic groups can be made up of apathetic individuals, of course, but more likely the apathy is a result of structural problems (Fisher, 1980).[13] The task may be perceived as unimportant and not worth the effort, or so difficult as to appear overwhelming. Sometimes groups lack the essential knowledge or skills to do the task, or they may not know what is expected. As with conflict, apathy needs to be identified and addressed. Effective group participants spot it and ask what is needed to rekindle enthusiasm.

- *Groupthink.* Groupthink occurs when group members fail to disagree when they should disagree. The term was coined by sociologist Irvin Janis (1972)[14] when he studied decision-making processes of American presidential advisory groups. Without healthy disagreement there is often premature agreement on one solution—sometimes the wrong solution—before other options have been considered. A good facilitator can spot groupthink, but so can alert members of the group. The thing to do is to play devil's advocate and raise "what-if" questions.

- *Social loafing.* Sometimes group members don't do their part or carry their own weight. Old experiments with tug-of-war games showed that two don't pull twice as hard as one, and three don't pull three times as hard, etc. Sociologists call this "social loafing," shirking responsibilities and letting other members carry the task (Pavitt and Curtis, 1990).[15] The group leader, if there is one, needs to know if this is happening. Usually, however, the leader will turn the problem back to the group—so it may be best for group members to identify the problem and confront the social loafer first. Serious loafing will affect the group's productivity, morale, and possibly your own learning in the group.

All of these problems are natural, but they need to be addressed. Responsibility for fixing these problems lies with the facilitator, but the solutions will ultimately need to come from members of the group.

Time Out

The next morning of the workshop is devoted to dealing with deeper feelings in groups. Yuko is terrified. Is she going to be required to share some deep, dark secret? Richard says he doesn't have any secrets because he has told them all. You suggest to Yuko that it may be best just to talk about her shyness, to see if others experience what she feels and if they have any suggestions. The facilitator opens with some comments to prepare participants for a different kind of group experience.

GOING DEEPER
Emotional Learning

Sometimes groups are used in organizational settings for human relations training. Social service organizations may use groups for purposes that approach those of group therapy. In this book, we are interested in groups for learning, not therapy, but the line between these purposes is not always clear. Sometimes groups go deeper into fairly sensitive emotional learning. What is your role when this is the purpose of the group?

Everything said about groups still applies. In addition, there is a deeper analysis of feelings, interactions, and perceptions that will take place. In the words of Carl Rogers, one of the originators of groups designed for personal growth, "The individual comes to know himself and each of the others more completely than is possible in the usual social or working relationships. He becomes deeply acquainted with the other members and with his own inner self, the self that otherwise tends to be hidden behind his facade."[16] Such groups can provide a useful laboratory for learning or relearning of emotional issues—a deeper strata of opinions, attitudes, and beliefs.

The first choice you have is whether you want to participate in such groups or not. If not, you have a right to make that clear and withdraw without embarrassment. If you decide to get involved, there are things to know about this kind of learning that can help you get the most out of it.

Irvin D. Yalom, the author of an important text on group therapy, *The Theory and Practice of Group Psychotherapy* (1985),[17] notes eleven "therapeutic" factors that make therapy in groups effective. These factors are paraphrased here and provide a good list of the kinds of outcomes you might expect from participating in groups that go deeper.

1. *Instillation of hope.* People who share a problem come to believe there is hope for resolving it.

2. *Universality.* Participants realize they are not alone and that others have a similar problem.

3. *Imparting information.* Members of the group share information about how they have dealt with the problem.

4. *Altruism.* People discover that they can be helpful to others.

5. *Recapitulation of the family.* Groups become like families and members rediscover how they have acted as family members.

6. *Development of social skills.* Members become aware that they are perceived as shy, regal, tactless, or aggressive, and learn new interpersonal skills.

7. *Imitative behavior.* Participants imitate the positive behaviors of the facilitator and of other group members.

8. *Interpersonal learning.* Members can have a corrective emotional experience where they review critical incidents in their lives and where they relearn something about relationships.

9. *Group cohesiveness.* A sense of good feeling among group members provides the therapeutic setting for acceptance and honest sharing of feelings.

10. *Catharsis*. The group becomes a place where members can get things off their chest, and this in itself can be therapeutic.

11. *Existential factors*. Participants get a new sense of what life is all about and learn to live life more honestly.

Not all of these factors will be present in every group, but in general these are the outcomes to anticipate. Seen in this way, groups that go deeper are not really so scary, and provide some opportunities for relevant and meaningful learning—something that can make a difference in your life—that other ways of learning may not provide.

Most groups that deal with this kind of learning are led by skilled facilitators. It is helpful to you as a participant if you understand some of the things the facilitator is trying to do.

- *Deepening the communication*. The facilitator will set certain guidelines for deeper communication, such as active involvement, nonjudgmental acceptance of others, and open self-disclosure. The facilitator may provide an instrument or activity, but may also just define an issue or topic and open the discussion. The facilitator will also model the desired communication patterns. Your job is to help this process by being honest in your own statements and by being an active listener, at a deeper level, for others.

- *Focusing on the here and now*. Although many forms of individual therapy focus on digging up the past, there is a strong tradition in groups to focus on the present. This includes not only the real problems of group members' present lives in a relevant context, but the real communication events taking place while the group is in progress. The interactions of the group members in any present moment will become a significant part of the discussion, and you can watch for and anticipate—you may even get caught up in—an analysis of the present communication exchange taking place in the group. For example: "Yes, this overdependent attitude that you say is a problem for you seems to be showing up for you now in the way you are looking toward all of us for some sort of solution."

- *Looking for learning.* The facilitator will be looking for recurrent themes, the feelings that get identified and repeated, and you should be doing that, too. Sometimes this is called *process commentary.* The facilitator will comment on the themes and meanings that are surfacing in the group. Sometimes the facilitator, without being judgmental, will point out how a member's behavior (maybe your own) makes others feel, or how the behavior brings about certain reactions from others. These are the little "aha" moments when deeper learning can occur. Something inside gets jarred and realigned. Watch for them, listen carefully, and try to learn from them. Look for these key moments in the group and ask yourself: What can I learn from that? If you were involved in some significant way, ask yourself: What did I learn from that? Write it down. Continue to think about it during the day or later in the week. Groups that go deeper often result in reexamination of fundamental beliefs or attitudes, and this is sometimes painful, but the learning that takes place can be extremely valuable.

Time Out

At first everyone stares at the floor. The facilitator waits, then eventually says, "Don't be shy." Yuko blurts out, "But I am." She sees other heads nodding sympathetically and realizes she is not alone. Without meaning to, she has established the first topic for the session. But because she recognizes that others are shy, too, she is not as fearful as she was. She begins to describe her family, the small town where she grew up, the cultural characteristics of Japan that teach girls to be quiet, reserved, and embarrassed. She listens to other group members tell their stories, and she is impressed at how supportive the facilitator is and how insightful the other group members are.

LEARNING TEAMWORK
High-Performance Collaboration

Groups are also used to teach teamwork. Not all groups are teams, but teams have most of the characteristics of groups. One might say a team is a group with a mission. Teams require high levels of collaboration and usually this needs to be learned.

Time Out

The final activity of the workshop is a team-building exercise. Participants are divided into teams of ten and work on a simple apparatus where each member of the team must be slid face-down across a smooth 2" x 12" plank, 10 feet long. If any person hits the surrounding, low-lying ropes while participants are being slid across the board, the whole team has to start over from the beginning. The race is against the clock.

The activity proves to be harder than it looks, and because people come in various shapes and sizes, true teamwork is required for pushing and tugging individuals from one end of the plank to the other.

The following is what the facilitator concludes about teamwork. After studying many types of teams in a variety of work settings, Carl Larson and Frank LaFasto (1989)[18] developed a list of the characteristics of high-performance teams. They concluded that teams need a "clear and elevating goal," that they must be composed of "competent members" who are able to develop a "unified commitment" and a "results-driven structure" that provides a "collaborative climate." They also need "principled leadership" that helps the team set "standards of excellence," and they thrive best when there is "external support and recognition." The authors also discovered (39–58)[19] that there are different types of teams—problem-solving teams, creativity teams, and tactical teams—and that the composition, structure, and working environment needed by the different types varies.

If you are on a team, you and the other team members need to be clear about what type of team this is, what the purposes are, and what kind of collaboration best serves the purposes of the team.

Sometimes you and the team may be working together through an activity that appears not to have any direct relation to what the team actually does in a work setting; for example, working on "ropes" on an apparatus high off the ground. The initial reaction is to think, What good is this weird stuff? Remember, like much instrumented group work, teamwork activities are often a metaphor for other behaviors, such as goal setting, cooperation, courage, support, and communication. You learn *through* the activity, and if you are confused at the end, ask for clarification: What was it we were learning?

LESSONS LEARNED

Ten Things You Can Do to Maximize Your Learning

1. Ask what kind of learning can come from this group.

2. Understand the organizational arrangements.

3. Know the task or purpose of the group activity.

4. Participate actively in the process in appropriate ways.

5. Know your niche and play your role.

6. Be willing to share your ideas and feelings.

7. Be an active listener and show that you are listening.

8. Notice nonverbal behavior.

9. Watch for, identify, and do something about problems.

10. Ask for clarification about intended learning.

IMPROVING PERFORMANCE
· ·
Learning Through Virtual Realities

WE SPEAK ABOUT THE "REAL WORLD" as if there were some other world that isn't real. The real world suggests harshness and toughness. We say, "She needs a good dose of reality." In our everyday speech we make the distinction between the real world and more sheltered environments.

Some jobs are hard to learn in the real-world setting where they are performed, because making a mistake can be costly or even life threatening. Sometimes large sums of money or physical safety are at stake. In military or emergency preparedness training, one hopes never to use what was learned. For these situations, learning in virtual realities is a welcome alternative to the real situation.

WHEN PRACTICE MAKES PERFECT
The Need for Virtual Realities

Virtual means existing in effect but not in fact. When we look in a mirror we see what the field of optics has long called a *virtual image*. Virtual realities are simulated environments for learning.

The degree to which the virtual environment imitates the real environment can vary, ranging from a simple classroom role play to the high-tech simulated cockpits for training pilots. The most typical activities for learning are role plays, dramatic scenarios, and simulations. As with other ways of learning, knowing how to participate can help you maximize your learning.

Role plays, dramatic scenarios, and simulations are carefully designed to bridge the real world of a job setting and the virtual world of a learning environment. Key elements of the real world have been selected, rearranged, and often compressed, to create a situation where participants can gain better understanding of their roles, display and practice abilities actually needed to perform their roles, and gain insights about themselves as the players of those roles.

Learning through virtual realities can be seen in the folk models of primitive societies with their games of strategy and chance, various dramatic enactments, and ceremonies designed to express social relations (Moore and Anderson, 1975, 49–50).[1] The roots of the use of role play and dramatic scenarios as methods of education and training are found in the work of J.L. Moreno (1889–1974), an eccentric Viennese doctor now recognized as the undisputed founder of *psychodrama* and *sociodrama* (Marineau, 1989, 25–49).[2] The historical origins of simulations and games are found in the military sciences, particularly the war games of the nineteenth-century Prussian army (Jones, 1987).[3] Much of the theory comes from the study of sociodrama and psychodrama, but there is also a body of theory related to gaming and simulation.

Time Out

Imagine that you are reading this chapter on a late-night flight, sometimes called a "red-eye special." Because most of the passengers got off at the previous stop, the atmosphere has become rather informal on this final leg of the journey and you are able to befriend two of the flight attendants. You read some pages of this chapter and you wonder if they experienced this way of learning. You ask them questions about their training.

PRACTICING A TYPICAL ENCOUNTER
Role Playing

A role play is an activity where a limited number of participants, usually two or three, take on specifically assigned roles and act out an encounter that involves some goal or problem. For example, one player might take on the role of a dissatisfied customer returning a product, while the person playing the role of clerk is instructed to maintain an all-sales-final policy. The concept of *role* comes from the field of sociology and suggests "a cluster of socially prescribed behaviors associated with particular social positions" (Persell, 1989, 58).[4] Thus roles carry *social expectations,* though these will vary with the situation. Being a wife (or husband) is a role, but being a wife in Jeddah, Saudi Arabia, carries different social expectations than being a wife in Beverly Hills, California. Role plays are used for analyzing a role, teaching a role, practicing a role, or evaluating how well participants can play their role, so the first thing you should ask about a role play is its *purpose* (Shaw, et. al., 1979).[5] Whether you are a player or observer, you should be clear about why the role play is being used.

You should also be able to identify the type of arrangements for the role play (Cooke, 1987, 430–31).[6] Sometimes a *single role play* will be acted out in front of the participants, but at other times *multiple role plays* will be presented simultaneously. Sometimes the role play has *low structure* with only a general description of the situation provided to the players; at other times a *high-structure role play* may employ detailed and carefully crafted scripts. Occasionally the players will have *alter egos* or *coaches* assigned to help them play the role. Sometimes the *spoken dialogue* is the focus of the role play, but at other times the *nonverbal action* is the key. If you find yourself in a role play, ask about the arrangements and get clear in your own mind what the arrangements are.

The *materials* used to initiate a role play are similar to the instruments used for group activities. These materials are not so much instructions as efforts to create a setting or state of mind (Maier, et. al., 1975, 12).[7] Role play materials must emphasize roles—what people will do in a particular situation and how their efforts to play their roles will become complicated as the action progresses. You may encounter brief descriptions of the background or setting, sketches of the character you will play, suggestions about what you are to say, or actual scripts, short cases, or situations set up through in-basket memos or typical e-mail exchanges. The materials you receive probably will not be the same as the materials that other players receive, and often you will not know what they have been told to do. You should read your materials quickly but carefully and should be able to gain enough information to know how to play your role. In some instances you may receive verbal instructions or be asked to watch an initial demonstration. In any case, you need to be able to understand your role well enough to play it. If you are unclear, ask for help.

As you begin to play your role, look for the different aspects of the role that could be emphasized (Sternberg and Garcia, 1989).[8] Sometimes role plays are designed to illustrate *role conflict,* when social expectations pull the player in two different directions at once. Other role plays are designed to present a *new role* full of puzzles and surprises. At other times the emphasis is on *role relationships* and interaction and communication is the key. Other role plays emphasize *role fatigue,* situations where it is difficult to play the same role over and over again without tiring. Some role plays are designed to explore *role confusion* and its consequences. Role plays can also be designed to explore *dual roles,* when a person sometimes wears two hats. You may also be asked to play one role and then switch to your partner's role in what is called *role reversal.* Know the goal of your role.

Sometimes the role you are given is clear and well defined, perhaps even scripted. In this case you are *role taking,* and following instructions closely will be important. At other times you have more freedom to interpret the role and you are actually *role playing.* Sometimes you will be forced into *role creating,* where you have to improvise the role using a lot of inventiveness and spontaneity (Sternberg and Garcia, 1989).[9] You may feel shy or you may welcome the opportunity to be on stage; in either case remember that the purpose of role playing is to create a virtual reality. You need to avoid the extremes of a lifeless reading or an overacted melodrama. Play it straight, to the best of your ability. What would you really do and say if you were in that situation?

The best technology for a role play is a live camcorder video and an instant replay. You can learn about your role and how you played it by watching the video and discussing it with colleagues.

Time Out

You get up and wander back to where Vicki and Joe are chatting, and you tell them how impressed you are with the way flight attendants are able to deal with all kinds of people, including some very obnoxious passengers you have seen on crowded Friday night flights. You wonder if they practice any of this through role plays in their training. They look at each other and smile. "We role play everything," notes Vicki. "We role play passengers in wheel chairs, blind passengers, deaf passengers." Joe chimes in, "They also give us cross-cultural role plays of passengers from other countries with different customs." "Yes," says Vicki, "our trainers anticipate just about every situation we can encounter, and they don't just tell you about it, they expect you to practice and show you can handle it." You thank them and return to your seat to continue your reading.

DEALING WITH COMPLEX SITUATIONS
Dramatic Scenarios

Dramatic scenarios are enactments of more complex situations, usually involving several characters and a problem that unfolds or evolves, much like a short scene from a play. Dramatic scenarios have their roots in theories growing out of the study of *sociodrama* and *psychodrama*. The inventor of these techniques, J.L. Moreno, spent his lunch hours in a park in Vienna, perched in the crotch of a tree from which vantage point he could direct the play of the children by assigning parts and inventing stories for them to act out. When the authorities became concerned, he shifted his focus to adults and developed over the years (as he immigrated to the U.S.) dramatic techniques for psychotherapeutic and educational purposes (Marineau, 1989).[10]

Most dramatic scenarios involve roles, just as actors in a play take on roles, so that everything that was said previously about role playing also applies to dramatic scenarios. What makes a dramatic scenario different is the length of the action and the complexity of the situation. In most cases there are several players and some observers.

Like a role play, a dramatic scenario needs something to get it started. There is a scene to be enacted; hence the term *scenario*. In some cases the scenario will be carefully worked out ahead of time, with suggested dialogue for each player, a description of the scene, a summary of the action, and perhaps even props and costumes. At other times the preparation will be less formal and you will need to invent your lines and the actions, as in improvisational theater. In any case you need to be as clear as possible about your niche in this little drama so that you can craft your role realistically and convincingly.

An effective facilitator will lead you through the three stages typically used in sociodrama: *warming-up,* a time of preparation devoted to understanding the roles and the overall scenario; *enactment,* the actual portrayal of the situation; and *sharing,* the occasion after the enactment for exchanging ideas and feelings among participants and observers (Sternberg and Garcia, 1989).[11] Learning usually takes place both at the time of enactment and through the sharing afterward.

The facilitator, if knowledgeable about dramatic scenarios, can use various techniques to enhance the enactment and the learning that flows from it. Watch for the following (Sternberg and Garcia, 1989, 55–69).[12]

- *Role change.* Players are shifted from part to part so they can experience different perspectives.

- *Double.* An additional player is used to express the inner thoughts or real feelings of one of the players.

- *Mirror.* A double takes another player's place temporarily to enable that player to step out and watch. Sometimes the facilitator will act as the mirror.

- *Empty chair.* An imaginary extra player provides the players a third party to experiment with, or vent their feelings on.

- *Soliloquy.* As in a play, a player steps back from the action to express inner feelings and thoughts.

- *Freeze frame.* The facilitator stops the action (as with a video) and comments on the body language, expressions, tone of voice, communication, and arrangement in space of the players.

- *Concretization*. Abstract expressions like "bouncing off the walls" are played out as concrete actions that represent feelings.

- *Sculpting*. The facilitator arranges a whole scene to portray actual relationships; for example, a dependent person clinging to the knees of another.

- *Future projection*. The facilitator asks the players to play out this scene at some future point in time.

With these techniques in mind you will not be surprised at what you and other players are asked to do. If you wish, you might ask the facilitator to use one or more of these techniques at some appropriate point or you may employ one of these techniques yourself, such as a soliloquy, to add interest to your part.

Videotape is also a useful technology for dramatic scenarios, and the ultimate arrangement is to have a studio with two cameras and a mixer.

Time Out

You are overcome with curiosity so you get up from your seat and make your way back to the flight attendants' station. You tell Vicki and Joe what you have been reading about and ask if anything like this is used in their training. "Oh, of course," says Vicki. "You mentioned those difficult passengers who present inappropriate behaviors. The trainers give us those situations." Joe enters in, "Everyone has their script and usually in those situations there is more than one thing happening, so the whole crew has to respond. When you actually encounter something like that, you know you can handle it because you have practiced." Vicki notes, "These are not easy. They are very challenging and realistic." You thank them and return to your seat, ready to read on.

ALMOST BETTER THAN REALITY
Simulations and Games

The terms *simulation* and *game* are often used interchangeably and sometimes the term *simulation game* combines both. Simulations are representations of some aspect of the real world where abstract models are developed and then manipulated in dynamic ways to create learning (Barton, 1970).[13] Simulation involves abstracting elements of a social or physical reality so that a person can enter into it and learn (Dukes and Seidner, 1978).[14] A game is a type of simulation that stresses competition among adversaries, a contest with rules and clear outcomes (Abt, 1970).[15] Although in most simulation games the players or groups of players compete against each other, sometimes they work together against a common adversary or to control a natural event or destructive force. Not all simulations are games, because some lack a competitive element. And not all games are simulations, because some are played just for entertainment. Simulations and simulation games provide serious opportunities for learning.

If you find yourself involved in a simulation or simulation game, you can orient yourself by remembering the eight R's of simulation (Davis and Davis, 1998)[16]:

1. *Reasons*. Simulations have a purpose. Ask yourself: What are the reasons for this activity?

2. *Reality*. An aspect of reality is being portrayed. What aspects of reality are being stressed through this simulation?

3. *Roles*. People will take on roles, but their roles are related to the object of the simulation or the niche they serve in the game.

4. *Rules*. The activity will have certain rules or procedures that set the parameters. Know the rules! Can they be broken? Who enforces them? Will there also be elements of chance?

5. *Resources*. Some simulations are simple; others require elaborate resources, such as an apparatus, data banks, objects,

pre-recorded videos, and other materials and supplies. What resources will you have to work with?

6. *Records*. As the activity unfolds you may need places to store or further analyze data. What records will be kept and who will keep them?

7. *Running time*. The activity will probably have certain steps and phases, and you should have a general idea of the time allotted.

8. *Results*. The activity will produce certain results, winners and losers, or a resolution of some type. When that happens, you know the simulation is finished and it is time for debriefing.

The facilitator usually plays a behind-the-scenes role with a simulation, particularly if it is a game (Jones, 1987).[17] The facilitator will select the simulation or create it, identify and assign participants and observers, generate materials, obtain space, and provide an initial briefing. Beyond that, the facilitator plays the role of detached observer, usually refusing to answer questions or give advice. The reason for this is that a good simulation should be designed in such a way that it can run almost unassisted. The participants should own the activity and the mood should go uninterrupted, thus heightening the semblance of reality. Facilitators who appear remote are doing their jobs. Don't bother them.

Afterward, however, the facilitator will probably initiate a debriefing. If not, you should ask for one. You can help the facilitator with the debriefing and help to maximize learning for others by moving beyond the immediate details and issues of the simulation or game to focus on the learning that occurred. You can ask: What did we learn from this?

Time Out

Vicki and Joe come up the aisle and they stop to chat with you about your reading. You tell them that you just finished a section on simulations and you ask them if the trainers use these. Vicki sits down next to you and Joe leans over the seat in front. "That's how we practice our emergency training," says Vicki. "We have a lot of lectures and things to learn from the manual, but you have to be able to do it." Joe adds, "You hope to never use it, but what the passengers expect of us is that we are ready if we have to deal with an emergency." Vicki points out, "We have the mock-up of an actual cabin and they put us in there and things start to happen. You need to know what to do, because afterward we talk about anything that went wrong or that could be improved." You thank them and ask if pilots have simulation training, too. They laugh, and Vicki says, "That's primarily how they are trained." Joe asks, "Would you like to talk to one of them about it?"

Simulations and games can range from a brief, focused game that runs a fraction of an hour to much longer and more complex arrangements. Some complex simulations use high-tech virtual realities with costly equipment coordinated by computers. Taped or filmed images are sometimes used with recorded sounds and operating controls that actually move parts of the apparatus. High-tech simulated environments are increasingly available, and using virtual realities will become a popular way of learning as new technologies continue to emerge.

Time Out

The pilot let you watch the first part of the landing approach and then he gave you his card and a number to call for a visit to the flight training simulation center. You followed up and joined a public relations tour. They even let you sit in one of those $19 million simulators and practice a landing approach. Wow! How exciting! Just like the real thing. You were so proud of yourself, banking on the approach, maintaining proper altitude, it seemed, right until the end. Then there was a big thump and everything went black. Back to reality.

LESSONS LEARNED
Ten Things You Can Do to Maximize Your Learning

1. Recognize when you need a safe environment for practice.

2. Learn how to participate effectively in role plays, dramatic scenarios, and simulations.

3. Know the different types and aspects of role plays and what they require.

4. Play your role realistically.

5. Craft your part creatively in a dramatic scenario and be aware of what other players are doing.

6. Know the facilitator's techniques for heightening the drama and increasing learning.

7. Note key elements in a simulation and help it unfold naturally without the facilitator's help.

8. Notice and learn to engage the technologies being used.

9. Ask what was learned and what still needs to be learned.

10. Know when you are ready to perform in the real world.

LEARNING FROM EXPERIENCE

Holistic Learning

E VERYONE LEARNS FROM EXPERIENCE, we say, but alas, we all know people who never seem to. Sometimes we look back and say, "That was a painful experience, but actually it was a good learning experience." We often mention "learning" and "experience" in the same breath.

A great amount of learning takes place outside of classrooms or formal training environments simply through experience. Many colleges and universities today urge students to have a cooperative education experience, a wilderness challenge experience, or a study abroad experience, and for such experiences the term *experiential learning* is used. In organizational settings this type of learning is sometimes known as *action learning*. We prefer the term *experience-based learning* and use it to refer to sponsored or guided experiences identified or established for the express purpose of bringing about learning. In most cases this involves procedures for selecting and assigning the experience, planning for it, supervising it, and making provisions for participants to reflect on the experience.

Experience-based learning has its foundation in holistic learning theory. *Holistic* refers to a way of learning that involves the whole person—sight, sound, touch, taste, and smell, as well as mind, emotions, body, and soul—simultaneously (Flake, 1993).[1] This way of learning is holistic because it reflects the capacity of the brain to take in and synthesize many aspects of experience at once.

Holistic learning theory has its origins in modern brain research. Of all the ways of learning, it is based on the most recently developed theory. Neuropsychologists who study brain anatomy and function suggest that human beings are "efficient, multitrack simultaneous processors," which is a sophisticated way of saying holistic learners. Holistic education is now a national movement in the United States, but it has its roots in the thought of John Dewey and Alfred North Whitehead, both of whom believed strongly in using experience to promote learning (Gang, 1993[2]; Hendley and Dewey, 1986[3]). Theories that elaborate on reflection as a technique to support learning from experience grow out of clinical research in counseling psychology.

Time Out

Surely every adult has had the experience of an overnight hotel stay. Sometimes several things happen to make it a particularly good or bad experience, but we don't usually think of staying in a hotel as an opportunity for learning. Consider the possibility, however, that you are an employee of a hotel and the manager has selected you and two others, Jeff and Anna, to go and stay in your competitor's hotel across town to learn what it is like to be a guest in that hotel. What is different about just being a guest in a hotel and actually trying to learn from the experience?

THE CIRCLE OF EXPERIENCE
Reflection-in-Action

How is raw experience used for learning? The answer to this question is found in the work of David Kolb (1984, 22–23),[4] who has developed a useful model for thinking about experience-based learning. This way of learning begins in concrete experience. First we have some experience, and as we have it we begin to reflect on what it means. As the *reflection* deepens, we begin to engage in *abstract conceptualization* about what has taken place. As we develop our ideas about the experience we feel the need to test these ideas to see if they are valid. This testing is done through a process of *active experimentation,* which of necessity returns us to *concrete experience.* Kolb's work suggests that learning from experience involves a cycle, some phases, a going out and coming back, and, above all, a process of reflection.

Is this way of learning merely the application of formal knowledge learned in classrooms to practical settings, or is there a new, perhaps qualitatively different kind of learning that grows out of experience? A case for answering yes has been made by Donald Schön (1983),[5] who has written on the need to restructure professional education. He suggests that learning in professional settings involves *reflection in action,* a way of knowing that grows out of experience. It is a kind of knowing that comes through our actions as *reflective practitioners* and is different from formal knowledge.

There is a commonsense resonance to the idea that we learn certain things from experience. It is doubtful that one can learn tightrope walking from a lecture on the subject. Some things we learn by doing. As with other ways of learning, understanding the theory will help you to know what you can do to maximize your learning from experience.

THE THREE-PART BRAIN
Wired for Holistic Learning

Neuropsychologists have gone one step beyond cognitive psychologists; they hope to learn about learning by studying the
brain directly. In recent years there has been an outpouring of
results of research on the brain—how it has evolved, what it
consists of, and how it functions. Classic summaries of that
research are found in Paul D. MacLean's *A Triune Concept of the
Brain and Behavior* (1973)[6] and in the late Carl Sagan's *The
Dragons of Eden* (1977)[7]. The picture that scientists paint is of a
triune brain with the three parts functioning as a whole but not
always in harmony. As the human brain evolved, three additional layers surmounted the spinal cord, each with its new functions but each also needing to accommodate the previous layer.
It is as if we have three different mentalities, two of which have
no speech (Sagan, 1977, 53, 57).[8] The three parts of the brain (not
to be confused with right and left hemispheres) can be distin-
guished anatomically, functionally, and neurochemically. Keep
in mind that all three layers are still present.

The human brain is not the largest brain overall in the animal
kingdom—it is roughly three pounds and a quart (1,500 grams
and a liter)—but it is the most developed and highly complex
of the animal brains. Human brains are, on average, six times
larger relative to body weight than the brains of other animals.
(Dolphins are notable big-brain exceptions.) If a giraffe can be
thought of as a "neck freak" and an elephant as a "nose freak,"
human beings are "brain freaks" (Sagan, 1977, 35).[9] The process
of brain enlargement, known as *encephalization,* occurred to
accommodate language—and ultimately the capacity for intelligent behavior—not only for communication but to develop the
words and images to map the territory of human experience
(Jerison, 1977, 42ff).[10]

Although the three parts of the brain do not always get along together, an important finding of this recent research is that the brain is extremely "well wired" (Fishbach, 1994).[11] Our 100 billion brain cells (about as many as there are stars in the Milky Way) are quite specialized, but they work together in banks. One of the reasons the cerebral cortex is so concentrated and convoluted—it would occupy 1.5 square meters if it were stretched out—is to facilitate connections among brain cells.

The brain is not just an isolated organ; it is connected to the world of experience through the senses and is able to function as both a sender and receiver (Sylwester, 1995).[12] Although the sense organs work independently, they also function simultaneously. Much of the brain's sensory and motor activity is automatic, managed by the cerebellum and basal ganglia, so that other parts of the brain are freed for simultaneous seeing, hearing, thinking, and communication activities. Apparently we are wired for holistic learning.

Leslie Hart (1983),[13] in his fascinating book, *Human Brain and Human Learning,* spells out the implications of recent brain research for learning. Humans learn, Hart contends, not in the logical, rational, linear mode of most classrooms. The human brain operates in a multilinear way all at once, using all of the sensibilities, employing its many layers, going down many paths simultaneously. In an instant we can identify an object by gathering information on size, shape, color, texture, weight, sound, movement, and so forth—the investigation proceeds along many paths at once. The brain's greatest ability is to make sense of the world by generating, storing, and calling forth programs to deal with experience.

To illustrate the point, Hart describes how children learn to play baseball not by lectures on the geometry of the playing field or even by systematic development of throwing, catching, hitting, and running skills, but rather by experiencing the game and picking it up over time. Human beings, both children and adults, seem to pick up learning in a somewhat random, happenstance manner from all kinds of exposures to experience.

Frank Smith (1990),[14] a noted psychologist and author of a well-known text on reading, suggests in his book, *To Think,* that learning should be thought of as a natural, commonplace process rather than a matter of deliberate intention. "The brain picks up huge amounts of information incidentally," Smith notes, "the way our shoes pick up mud when we walk through the woods" (12).[15] Smith also asks: "If learning is normally so easy, why should it sometimes be so difficult?" Hart (1983, 109)[16] argues that learning becomes difficult when there is too much structure, and particularly when there is pressure. When the organism is under threat, the older brain takes over and our panic makes us freeze and leaves us literally speechless. Hart calls this automatic response of the brain "downshifting." Under pressure in classrooms, something can "snap." Have you ever had that experience? The ideas of Hart and Smith support holistic learning through experience in natural environments.

Time Out

The hotel across town provides a natural environment for learning. There is no classroom, no textbook to be read, no surprise quizzes. Your well-wired brain is ready to see, hear, taste, smell, and touch whatever you encounter. What other natural environments—places to travel, things to see or do, adventures to experience—can provide opportunities for learning? Can you identify common, everyday experiences from which you could learn, if you thought of them as opportunities for learning?

INTERPRETING EXPERIENCE
Constructing Meaning

Holistic learning also receives support from a new group of philosophers and psychologists known as *constructivists*. Constructivists begin with the idea that knowledge is not a copy of reality; rather, knowledge is the outcome of efforts to construct the meaning of phenomena in our experience. We do this in many ways—through the fine arts and music, through mathematical and scientific symbol systems and the telling of stories—always with the goal of making meaning of experience (Smith, 1990, 126).[17]

Jacqueline and Martin Brooks present a vivid illustration of constructing meaning in their book, *The Search for Understanding: The Case for Constructivist Classrooms* (1993).[18] A young girl, whose only experience with water is with her bathtub and swimming pool, has constructed a particular concept of water. Water is calm and moves when she moves. But when she goes to the ocean and experiences the waves throwing her about and crashing on the shore, she has to construct a new meaning for water. Like this child, all of us must make new meanings as we have new experiences. As we encounter new experiences three things can happen (Fosnot, 1996, 13–14).[19]

1. *Assimilation*—absorbing new experiences into previously established frameworks of meaning

2. *Accommodation*—changing our interpretation to assign new meaning

3. *Differentiation and integration*—adjusting two or more sets of interpretations simultaneously

The constructivists call this process of adjustment and reinterpretation *equilibration*. Learning from experience is often like being thrown in the ocean.

FROM EXPERIENCE TO LEARNING
The Reflection Process

Learning from experience does not occur automatically just from being immersed in something different; it requires *reflection in action*. As you approach an experience that has high potential for learning—either an experience you have been assigned to or one of your own choosing—there are several questions you can ask that will help to maximize your learning:

- *Is this the right experience for you?* Does the experience provide actual opportunities for learning and is this the learning you are seeking? Does the opportunity present the right level of challenge and are you ready for it? Is this a good match?

- *What preparation is needed?* What are the likely opportunities for learning and how can you be ready for them? What should you look for or anticipate? What background will you need to take into the experience?

- *What are your goals?* What do you want to accomplish through the experience? What activities do you hope to complete and what do you expect to learn through these activities?

- *How will you document your experience?* Will you use a laptop to keep a log or diary? Will you obtain or copy key reports or correspondence? Will you take pictures, make videos, or record audiotapes? Will you file regular brief reports? Will you write a final summary or give an oral report at the end of the experience?

- *What senses will you call into action?* If the brain is a well-wired, multichannel processor, how can you use it best? How will you maintain your alertness to the main events and the small details that illuminate these events? What will you allow yourself to see, hear, and feel?

- *What will you do about the unfamiliar?* When you experience something new, or find something that doesn't fit with your previous mode of interpretation, what will you do about that?

How will you construct meanings and assimilate or adjust to the unexpected?

- *With whom will you talk about this experience?* Will someone serve as mentor, counselor, or animator of this experience for you? What role will your supervisor play? Will you talk to a neutral third party?

Time Out

You, Jeff, and Anna prepare for your hotel visit. You take notepads and a digital camera. You make a list of things you want to examine, which includes check-in procedures, bellhop services, room arrangement and cleanliness, room services, the restaurants, the bar, the shops. You divide up the assignments, decide which employees you want to observe closely, what pictures you want to take, and so forth. You know that when you return to your hotel, your manager will be expecting some sharp observations and detailed comments.

Perhaps the most important thing you can do, in addition to the activities suggested in the questions posed above, is to establish an ongoing, serious, one-on-one dialogue with someone who can help facilitate your reflection. You will be bombarded with a variety of perceptions and impressions generated by your senses and received by your brain. Remember, however, that the essence of learning from experience is in making meaning of experience, and sometimes that requires big adjustments. You can do some of this reflection by yourself, particularly as you try to put your experience into words through diaries and reports. The reflection process will go much deeper and will ultimately result in more learning, however, if you have someone to talk to who can facilitate your reflection.

What can you expect from these conversations? You can expect more if the person you are able to talk to has some skill as a facilitator. On the other hand, if no trained facilitator is designated or available, you can choose a person with good listening skills and discuss with them how they can help you meet your needs for reflection. At a minimum you should arrange for at least one conversation at the end of the experience, but your reflection will be enhanced greatly through several conversations while you are immersed in the experience. In this case the dialogue is not only about what is happening but what you can do about what is happening.

Facilitating reflection is like counseling. A standard textbook used in teaching counselors is Gerard Egan's *The Skilled Helper: A Systematic Approach to Effective Helping* (1990).[20] Your mentor in this situation may or may not know this book (or any other book on counseling), but together you can use the principles outlined in this book to frame your reflection process. Use these guidelines:

- *Tell your story.* Egan calls this the *present scenario.* As best you can, tell what is happening. Describe your experience in full detail. What are you seeing and hearing? What is your interpretation? Ask your mentor if this seems like an accurate description, and welcome a challenge if you are misinterpreting or leaving something out. Telling the story by putting your experience into words is in itself a valuable aid to learning, but as you tell the story some problem or concern is likely to arise. Ask yourself if everything is going okay and explore whether there is something you might be doing differently. The facilitator can help you define key issues and problems and help you to develop an initial assessment of the situation. What is missing, what needs to be explored further, what needs to be done?

- *Project a future.* Egan calls this the *preferred scenario.* Discuss with your mentor how you would like the situation to be. What would this situation look like if the problems were resolved and the missed opportunities were addressed? What are the other possible scenarios for this situation? What could be happening in your experience that is not happening now?

What accomplishments and changes would you like to see, not only for yourself but for the work and the people in that setting? This is your opportunity to dream a little and get beyond airing frustrations and complaints. Together, you and your mentor should be able to construct an agenda of things you can do before you meet again. Then you need to commit to doing some of the items on the agenda.

- *Implement your ideas.* Egan calls this *linking preferred scenarios to action strategies.* The focus is now on action. What are you actually doing in this situation to improve it, change it, or (more humbly) make your small contribution? What are your strategies for taking action? At this stage your conversation with your mentor can explore possibilities or, if you have already initiated some action, evaluate the consequences of your actions. Your dialogue will be filled with questions that begin: What if . . . ? Have I considered . . . ? Would it help if . . . ? Your goal here is to formulate plans, act on them, and then assess the outcomes of your action. Sometimes this is a painful business, but the person helping you with the reflection process can provide support and understanding if you are willing to be honest about the adjustments you are trying to make.

Time Out

When you, Jeff, and Anna return to your hotel, the manager is pleased with your well-documented observations. As you move through your report, the questions he raises are about how well your hotel performs compared to the hotel you visited. He asks about the areas of needed improvement and specifically what you think should be done to make changes. He wants to know if you are willing to put together a presentation to the entire staff on "The Customer's Viewpoint." After this experience, you realize that this is a valuable way of learning, but that you need to be systematic in making observations and reflective about what has occurred.

LESSONS LEARNED

Ten Things You Can Do to Maximize Your Learning

1. Identify experiences that provide potential for learning.

2. Make sure the experience is the right match for your learning needs.

3. Know how your brain is designed for holistic learning.

4. Awaken your senses and make systematic observations.

5. Search for and construct meaning.

6. Make preparations for the experience and set goals about what you hope to learn.

7. Be prepared to adjust to the new, different, and unexpected.

8. Write about and otherwise document the experience.

9. Seek a mentor to facilitate reflection.

10. Tell your story, project a future, take action, and ask what you learned.

PART THREE

. . . .

Maximizing Learning

11

HIGH-IMPACT LEARNING
. . . .
*Using the Seven Ways of Learning
to Get Results*

I N CERTAIN RESPECTS MANAGING IS LIKE COOKING: you need to select
the best ingredients and mix them together in just the right
amounts. Effective managers are good at selecting and mixing;
they know how to identify and use the right resources to get
results. As the manager of your own learning, you now have the
ingredients you need. You are aware of seven different ways of
learning and you know how to be an effective participant within the environment of each way.

The next step is to learn how to manage all the resources at
your disposal to get the best results. As you read this chapter you
will learn how to select appropriate ways of learning, how to use
them, and how to assess results.

CHOICE OR NO CHOICE
Getting the Most Out of Learning

When we place the seven ways of learning side by side, as we
have done in these chapters, the natural tendency is to ask:
Which theory is right? Which way of learning is best? If we have

learned anything together as the writers and readers of this book, it is that learning is a many-sided activity and there is no one "best way." The best way is the way that is most likely to bring about the results you want.

If you have a choice, you always want to select the way of learning that fits your desired learning outcomes. If your goal is to learn new skills, you need behavioral learning; if you want to understand and remember information, you need cognitive learning, and so forth. As obvious as this appears, people often make wrong choices for bad reasons.

There is a natural tendency to choose the way of learning you like most. That natural tendency has been reinforced recently by the popular interest in learning styles. For example, if you are an extrovert and you prefer learning in groups, it is natural that you would gravitate toward collaborative learning. It is natural to want to stay within your comfort zone. But if the learning you need and desire involves learning new skills, you will develop those skills most effectively and efficiently through behavioral learning, not through learning in groups. If you need to practice your performance, you need to learn through virtual realities, not through groups. A pilot will never learn to fly an airplane through learning in groups, however much he or she may prefer collaborative learning. On the other hand, passengers might learn to overcome their fear of flying through collaborative learning in groups. As the punishment fits the crime, so the appropriate way of learning should fit the desired outcome.

Can more than one way of learning be used? Yes and no. Different ways of learning can be used one after the other, and often are. In some classes or workshops several ways of learning might be used over one or two hours. You should be able to recognize different ways of learning and adapt quickly now. On the other hand, you cannot use two or more ways of learning to achieve *the same outcome*. Different ways of learning achieve different outcomes.

Time Out

Envision something you want to learn. Define specific outcomes. Which way of learning is best suited to those outcomes? If you need some review, go back to the Introduction to Part Two, pages 49–50, where you will find the lists of questions associated with each way of learning. If you still harbor some lingering belief that different ways of learning achieve the same outcome, reread any two of the ways of learning, compare them, and ask whether they achieve the same outcome.

An important challenge in managing your own learning is to choose and use the right way of learning for the right outcomes.

Sometimes you will have a choice about what to learn and how to learn it. If you have a choice, make a good match. If you have little or no choice and you find yourself assigned to a particular learning experience, your challenge is still to maximize your learning. The assigned experience may work out superbly for you and may prove to be just what you need, or you may dislike it intensely. In fact, you may dislike that way of learning and the way it is being carried out so much that you need to put forth high levels of effort in order to maximize the learning you can derive from that situation. Either way, selected or assigned, liking the experience or not, you have some degree of control over the situation.

You may also encounter situations that appear to be confusing or disorganized. When you have had good learning experiences you are not likely to be satisfied with less. In a sense, then, learning about learning is training for revolutionaries. Once you know how learning works—what the facilitator should be promoting and what you and the other participants should be doing—you will not find it easy to be a passive observer of a less-than-optimal experience. Now that you know about each way of learning, you also know how to improve the experience for yourself and others. You might protest, "It is not my responsibility to improve the learning experience; that's the facilitator's job." You may be right, but it is your role to get the most out of any learning experience even if that means helping to make the situation better. Many learning experiences could be improved dramatically by participants who have the knowledge and courage to improve them.

You can maximize your learning by making good choices about the way of learning or, when you have no choice, getting the most out of a situation that may be less than optimal. The focus is always on results.

LEARNING THAT STICKS
Intensity, Frequency, Duration

A lot of learning doesn't stick. You were there, you experienced the training, you sat through a class or workshop, you were exposed, but when it comes to recall, application, or real change of behavior or attitude, there is little impact. No results. Why is that?

Learning is like medicine; you have to follow the prescription carefully for best results. A man went to his doctor—so the story goes—and asked if there was any truth to the suggestion that stewed prunes will relieve constipation. The doctor replied in the affirmative. The man then asked the doctor how many prunes to eat. With a sly smile the doctor asked, "What kind of results do you want to get?" In prescribing medicine, physicians are accustomed to using three guidelines: intensity, frequency, and duration. *Intensity* refers to the level of dosage—the number of milligrams of the particular pill. *Frequency* refers to how often the pills are taken, for example, three times a day. *Duration* refers to the length of time of the course of administration, for example, one month. These terms—intensity, frequency, duration—are useful for thinking about how to maximize your learning.

There is a tendency, particularly in training programs where time away from the job and cost factors are important, to cut corners. Likewise, when we are pursuing our own learning independently there is a temptation to put in minimal time and effort because we face so many other demands on our time and energy. The problem with false economies is that they usually compromise results.

Intensity has to do with how well the way of learning is employed. If the experience is well designed and enthusiastically facilitated, and if you can clearly identify the way of learning and the theory behind it, the experience will probably have a high level of intensity. Each way of learning has its own internal ground rules for maximizing the intensity of the experience. Intensity grows out of the dynamic that occurs between facilitator and participant and among participants when everything is working as it should for that way of learning.

Frequency refers to how much time is allotted for each way of learning, how much the learning is practiced, and how many occasions might be necessary for real learning to occur. It is unlikely, for example, that you will learn much about problem solving from solving one problem, or a new skill with one try. Unfortunately, one-minute learning doesn't exist. Repeated exposure is often necessary.

Duration refers to how often the learning takes place over an extended period of time, how many times the learning can be revisited, and whether a sequence of learnings can be built one upon the other. Most learning takes time to process and absorb, so some types of learning may need to extend over several weeks or months to achieve high impact.

Time Out

Think of a learning experience where you actually did not learn very much. Was it the *intensity, frequency,* or *duration* that posed the problem, or was it all three? What should have happened?

The seven ways of learning offer no miracle cures and there is nothing magical about their use. They need to be engaged in rigorously, often enough, and over a long enough period of time to bring about desired results. Learning sticks when it is engaged in with appropriate intensity, frequency, and duration.

SELF-ASSESSMENT
Knowing What You Learned

Most of us learned to hate tests in school. Tests, we believed, were given to find out what we didn't know. Even a perfect paper sometimes came back marked "minus zero." The whole arrangement provokes embarrassment—someone who supposedly knows a lot, testing someone who hardly knows anything—so it is not surprising that we would rather not know what we learned than to have to take a test.

Knowing what you learned, however, is another important factor in managing your own learning. Is there some way to assess what you learn without always having to take a test? Sometimes tests are necessary, but we prefer to use the term *assessment* to get beyond the old ideas of testing and evaluation. We also prefer with adult learners to put the responsibility for finding out about what was learned into the hands of the learner. *Self-assessment* is simply knowing how well you learned. Self-assessment breaks up that treacherous game of trying to fool someone about what you don't know. The alternative to self-assessment is self-deception.

Sometimes the facilitators of the learning experience in which you are engaged may be conducting assessments. They may be following a familiar four-step model (Kirkpatrick, 1996)[1] where they want to know if you were *satisfied* with the learning, if actual *learning* took place, how much your *behavior* changed, and whether there were *results* for the organization. This is important information for trainers to gather, and you should cooperate with their efforts, but the goal of self-assessment is to provide the information you want about your own learning. The assessment you conduct can be formal or informal, it can draw on information you gather or the facilitator gathers, and it can be planned ahead of time or improvised later. In any case, you need to set up some arrangements for self-assessment for these three important reasons.

1. *You definitely need to know what you learned and how well you learned it.* These are your results. They tell you whether you need to try again or whether you are ready for additional learning.

2. *Assessment often provides feedback that is essential for the learning process itself.* For some ways of learning, feedback is actually a part of the learning process.

3. *Most people learn more if they know that someone is checking.* You are the one to check, of course, so you are playing a little game with yourself, but it's an honest game and you won't want to disappoint yourself.

The assessment strategies you design for yourself should be tailored specifically to each of the ways of learning. We can provide suggestions to get you started, but you should be inventive in designing assessment that fits the subject matter, the strategy, and your need for feedback.

1. *Learning new skills.* This way of learning is useful for building skills, so the assessment is really quite simple: Can you
   perform the skill? If the learning outcome is observable behavior, as it usually is in this case, then you need to observe your
   performance or work with someone who can give you that
   feedback. Behavioral learning usually involves steps, so if you
   can't perform the entire skill, perhaps you can assess which
   parts of the skill you do well and where you may be having
   trouble. Remember that knowledge of results in the behavioral
   way of learning also serves as reinforcement. Assessment at
   each step of the way provides needed reinforcement as well
   as information about how to proceed.

2. *Learning from presentations.* This way of learning is valuable
   for understanding and remembering information from explanations and other forms of presentation. Because understanding and remembering are internal mental processes, as
   opposed to observable behaviors, assessments usually need to
   be written or oral so that you have a chance to demonstrate
   to yourself or someone else what you understand and remember. Many written materials provide study guides, questions for
   review, or an alternate form of a test. Where there is no examination, make up a test of essentials and take it. If specific terminology must be remembered, develop memory devices and
   check how well they work. If it is a process, write a narrative
   of it from memory and then check it against your notes. If it
   is a product or service procedure, write a description or draw
   a diagram of it. You may prefer to tell someone what you have
   learned and then check on what you included or omitted. In
   any case, design an assessment that takes you beyond mental rehearsal and demonstrates openly, on paper or orally, that
   you understand and remember the essential information.

3. *Learning to think.* This way of learning helps to develop critical, creative, and dialogical thinking. Assessment will usually
   involve developing a written or oral critique of someone else's
   thinking or a report or proposal that represents your own
   thinking. An appropriate assessment might include an analysis of the way the argument is being made, the evidence, the
   assumptions, and the fallacies. Assessments for creativity

examine whether the ideas or products you or others have produced are new and appropriate. Dialogical thinking can be assessed by asking yourself to compare and contrast differing arguments, to generate counter-arguments, or to take an unfamiliar or uncomfortable position and defend it.

4. *Learning to solve problems and make decisions.* This way of learning calls on you to demonstrate the ability to use mental models in solving problems and in making decisions that project outcomes as probabilities. The assessment requires practice with problems and decisions, either through prepared cases or the real problems and decisions that come up in the organization. These can be used to generate hypothetical problems and decision points to see how well you employ appropriate mental models. In this assessment you are interested especially in the processes you are using to arrive at solutions and decisions; that is, how your responses are being framed and the methods you are using to arrive at your conclusions. You may want to treat a situation that you face as a case, and conduct a formal case analysis or set up a formal decision model.

5. *Learning in groups.* This way of learning is useful for exploring opinions, attitudes, and beliefs, and for building collaboration skills. If a videotape of your training is available you can watch it, alone or with a mentor, to see what you notice about your participation. Self-assessment can focus on changes that may have occurred internally for you—a new awareness of something in yourself or others, a changed attitude, or a modified belief. You may notice new communication or collaboration skills that you are bringing to your workplace group or team. You can ask colleagues if they notice any changes in you, and you can monitor your own group participation carefully. In general, the learning outcomes from groups and teams may be less tangible than from other ways of learning, so it may be especially important to ask yourself if you can put into words what you learned.

6. *Learning to perform.* This way of learning enables you to practice tasks that might otherwise have high risk in real life. The assessment involves seeing how close you can come to the

desired live performance. Unlike other forms of assessment where it is necessary to step back and do some additional activity to see if learning occurred, in this instance the learning is demonstrated in the performing. The role plays, dramatic scenarios, and simulations are the assessment. Presumably practice makes perfect, so the key to assessment here is in gaining feedback from the facilitator and the other participants about your performance. What you hope to uncover are the strengths and weaknesses in your performance, and the critical points at which improvements could be made.

7. *Learning from experience.* This way of learning uses all of the senses and the multitrack processing capabilities of the brain to pull learning out of experience. The assessment should address the question: What did you learn from this particular experience? Because this way of learning is enhanced through reflection, the various types of mechanisms you use—talking with a mentor, writing about your experience, or presenting your experience to others—are all rich in opportunities for self-assessment. Your efforts to make meaning of your experience are the assessment.

Efforts to assess your learning should be driven by the way of learning itself. Avoid inappropriate assessment methods—for example, testing factual recall to see what was learned from a group process, or testing problem-solving ability when the goal was only to understand and remember the information. Make sure that the assessment fits the learning, is representative of the total range of things learned, is of the right level of difficulty, and produces results that are actually useful to you in some important way.

Time Out

Think of a formal or informal learning experience you were engaged in recently. Did you learn anything? How do you know? Could you design some activities for assessing more carefully your learning in that situation? What would you do?

Managing your own learning also involves taking charge of the overall arrangements for learning. This includes, when you have a choice, selecting the right way of learning for getting desired results. When you have no choice, it means finding ways to maximize your learning anyway. It also includes managing the intensity, frequency, and duration of the experience for high impact, and assessing carefully what learning has taken place. Like a good cook, you will select the right ingredients for learning, use them in proper amounts, mix them expertly, and check frequently for taste.

12

SOURCES OF INFORMATION

Finding What You Need

"JUST GIVE ME THE COLD, HARD FACTS," some people say. Others say, "Don't confuse me with the facts." Although we have made the case that learning is more than remembering facts, we have never suggested that there is no relation between learning and information. Now that you understand learning more fully in its many variations, it is important to examine more carefully the role of information in learning. Learning always has some subject matter and usually involves information in either central or peripheral ways. Learning is always about something.

Another important aspect of managing your own learning is managing your information needs. In this chapter, you will learn how to improve your ability to seek and find information in libraries and on the Internet.

Each of the seven ways of learning has its own unique way of drawing on information. In learning skills through behavioral learning, for example, the skills always exist within some context of activity and it is usually necessary to have information about that activity. Sometimes the skill itself involves the intake or manipulation of information. In the cognitive way of learning information is attended to, processed, and remembered. Infor-

mation processing is central to that way of learning; a presentation has content. In the case of inquiry learning, participants are
always thinking critically, creatively, or dialogically about some
body of information. They may need more information. And so
forth. The role of information in each learning process is slightly different but never completely absent. You are either already
dealing with information—sound, relevant, or questionable—or
you are inspired to seek new information.

People who facilitate learning—teachers, trainers, professors—
are programmed to talk about the subject. Attorneys love to talk
about torts and contracts, engineers are eloquent about the
properties of metals, and artists speak passionately about line
and color. Talking about the process of learning is more difficult,
both for teachers and for learners. For that reason, as we
described the seven ways of learning presented in the chapters
in Part Two, we emphasized the *process* of learning. In doing so,
we may have underemphasized content, but we assume that
most readers can fill in appropriate subjects from their own field
for each way of learning.

Time Out

Think about something you intend to learn. Is there a subject content? In what ways is information involved? Do you have the needed
information? If not, where will you find it? Do you know how to find
it?

The most important thing to recognize about learning and
information is that the relationship today is almost the opposite
of what it was before the new era arrived. In the traditional
school or university programs that most of us experienced, information was brought to us. Today the situation is reversed:

instead of sitting passively waiting (often in vain) for the right information to drift by, learners in the new era must actively seek the information they need.

SEEKING INFORMATION
Using Libraries

Information can be found in many places, of course, in news-papers and magazines, in documents and reports at the work-place, and on the Internet (see page 180). But the best place to seek reliable and useful information is still in your nearby library.

Whatever image you may hold of libraries, be aware that libraries today are not what they used to be. A modern, up-to-date library still contains books and periodicals, with hardcopy collections varying in size and purpose according to the mission of that library, but the essence of a library today is networked informa-tion services. The way in which libraries operate has changed greatly in the last quarter century.

The first big change is the emphasis on *services*. To prepare yourself for a conversation with your librarian, try to formulate in your mind what question you are trying to answer and what information you need to answer it. Do you need historical back-ground or current data? Do you need scholarly books and arti-cles or popular magazines? Facts and figures or summaries and trends? Think of two or three key words that describe the areas in which you are searching. Never be ashamed of your lack of information or uncertainty. Librarians appreciate the complexity of the information maze, and know how to provide appropriate services to meet your needs.

Most libraries have a *reference* section, so before you begin to search for books or articles, consider whether someone already has assembled what you need in a review article, ency-clopedia, almanac, directory, annotated bibliography, or guidebook. Most reference information is in print, but materials also come in many other formats: microfilm, microfiche, CD-ROM, and online. The first stop in a library is the reference section.

The card catalog has been replaced with an online catalog accessed through a computer station or network of computers. If you don't know how to use the computer, ask the staff; they will help you or do it for you. If you know how to use the computer, you can access screens that will direct you to what the library contains. Each library has its own format for this, but in general you will find three pathways to information: the online catalog of materials owned by the library, electronic resources licensed by that library, and other materials including mediated access to information on the World Wide Web. Retrieval of information in all three areas may be accomplished by manipulating appropriate search mechanisms.

The path to books and periodicals is the online catalog of holdings for that library. If you are looking for particular books you can find them by title or author, but if you just have a topic you can search by subject using key words or subject headings. If the books and periodicals you want are not found in your library, remember that your library is probably part of a cooperative arrangement with other libraries called a *consortium* and the book can be borrowed from other libraries through interlibrary loan. Your library may also have readily available online catalogs of other libraries. Your librarian will know about your library's consortial connections. Some examples are the Michigan Library Consortium, the Colorado Alliance of Research Libraries, or the Consortium of Research Libraries, United Kingdom. Even small public libraries are linked to other libraries through state library systems in the United States (www. ohiolink.org). Many companies have corporate libraries and these are also linked to other libraries. Corporate libraries are usually members of the Special Libraries Association (www.sla.org). There is even a coalition of all the groups of libraries called the

International Coalition of Library Consortia (ICOLC). If you want to learn more about these cooperative arrangements among libraries you can access ICOLC by Internet at (www.library.yale.edu/consortia).

In recent years—this development is truly amazing—libraries have collaborated to produce an online database of their holdings—a master list, so to speak—of books in all participating libraries. Although not all countries are contributing to the system yet, the current list is more than adequate, truly international, and contains books in many foreign languages. This master catalog is coordinated by OCLC, the not-for-profit Online Computer Library Center (www.oclc.org) and is accessible as WorldCat. In most libraries access to WorldCat is limited to librarians because there is a cost for searching, but a librarian can tell you about literally any book in the world.

The second pathway to information is through licensed *electronic databases*. These are computer-based systems for searching for information by subject specialization or key word. Each library is licensed to use only certain databases—there is a cost to the library—but consortial memberships and licensing arrangements expand this access. An electronic database is a collection of information on a particular set of subjects; for example, education, business, or psychology, or more generally, the humanities. The managers of the database—sometimes called database vendors, electronic publishers, or suppliers—include the relevant periodicals, journals, and other materials for a set of fields and then index these materials by subject in very sophisticated ways, so that finding information by topic is swift and easy. Examples of database vendors are Academic Universe, Cambridge Scientific Abstracts, Galenet, OCLC, and Infotrac Search Bank. Each of the vendors makes available a particular combination of databases, and some databases are available through more than one vendor. Most libraries post a comprehensive list of the databases you can access at that library or through the consortium. You may not be able to tell what a database contains from its name, but you can enter a database electronically and find out. Your librarian can help you discover which databases are best for your interests, how to use their system of descriptors (key words), and how to find what you need.

The third pathway to information on the library computer screen leads you to information sources not in the online catalog. These may be nonprint resources, such as collections of videos or CDs, mediated websites, special collections, or archival collections. Sometimes very valuable instructional materials on how to use the library and its resources are provided on the library's Web pages.

Time Out

How would you rate yourself as a library user on a scale of 1 to 10, where 10 is every week? How would you rate your competence in using a modern, up-to-date library on a scale of 1 to 10, where 10 is highly competent? Do you have a good grasp of how to find the information you need most, or would it help to spend time in a library working with a librarian who can help you upgrade your skills?

NETWORKING FOR LEARNING
Using the Internet

The Internet is another source of information, but it also provides opportunities for lively discussions of controversial issues. It is a paradise for inquiring minds. The Internet is essentially a network of big and small computers that all speak a common language. *Internet* is the generic term used to describe what has now become the vast array of client and server computers and the phone lines, fiber-optic cables, and satellites that connect them. The Internet makes available several services, including the World Wide Web, electronic mail, newsgroups, listserves, and live conferencing capabilities. Although the Internet is immensely popular, the quality of the information is sometimes regarded as suspect because there are few freely accessible copyrighted or licensed materials and no controls comparable to the scholarly review processes for books and articles in journals. The information the Internet provides is different from that usually found in libraries, and it is best to think of it that way.

If you are seeking current information, particularly the kind of information a specific organization would have, you may be able to find it at a website. Websites are the electronic spaces that organizations create to post information. Websites have an address called a uniform resource locator (URL). Websites are part of the World Wide Web, hence the frequent abbreviation www as part of the address. Websites vary, of course, in what is posted, and they change regularly or grow out of date. Organizations post what they think the visiting public might be interested in, and their websites contain what they want you to know.

The Internet has its own search and metasearch mechanisms for finding websites, just as libraries have methods of searching for books and articles. Search mechanisms help you find websites that may fit your interests. For example, (to work backwards in this explanation) museums all over the world—art, natural history, science and industry, historical, and so forth— have stimulating websites that contain interesting information about their collections, often accompanied by pictures or displays, articles, research, bibliographies, or biographies of artists, scientists, or historical figures. Assume, for example, that you are searching for information about the history of air and space travel and you remember (or guess) that there is a museum devoted to the subject in Washington, D.C. You want to find that museum website. You go to one of the search mechanisms, such as AltaVista (www.altavista.com) and begin your search. You might know the name of the museum or you might search by topic or location. You may find various directories of museums, perhaps one for *Museums in Washington, D.C.* On the other hand, you may arrive at the site you are seeking through a completely different route. If you are persistent, eventually you will find the National Air and Space Museum and a link to their website (www.nasm.sci.edu). There you will find a menu from which you can select a heading that is likely to lead to the information you are seeking, such as *Collections and Research*.

Sometimes you may only have in mind a few key words to describe a broad topic. If you enter words for your search that are too general you can be presented with an unworkable number of websites, but if that happens the search mechanism also will provide suggestions for refining your search by requiring or excluding suggested words. Search mechanisms on the Internet are used to find websites.

Search mechanisms are of basically three types. *Search engines* using *spiders* or *crawlers* constantly visit websites on the Internet and automatically catalog what is there. AltaVista is an example of a search engine. *Directories,* unlike search engines, are created by humans, who receive submissions from websites and then assign them to appropriate categories. Yahoo is an example of a directory. *Hybrid search engines* are search engines that have an associated directory in which certain sites have been reviewed and rated. Lycos is an example of a hybrid search engine; it has associated directories and a rating service called "Top 5%" that reviews what is best on the Web.

The information on websites is scanned by search mechanisms for key words, focusing on the location of those words (the title, the first paragraph) and frequency of use. The search process, therefore, is essentially a matter of matching up the words you enter with the key words under which the website has been indexed. Different search mechanisms, therefore, will deliver sources of information in slightly different packages and will provide different services. When you arrive at the initial screen of a search mechanism, you will find a box where you can type in key words, or you can search within a specified menu of categories, such as travel, entertainment, news, and so forth. You will also spot advertisements for commercial products and services on the screen, as well as services that operate like a subscription with a monthly fee. The whole system is fairly recent, with some of the oldest search mechanisms dating back only to 1994.

The companies that provide search mechanisms buy other companies and are bought, and services are recombined, so anything written about them can become quickly out of date. If you wish to remain current about them look for *Search Engine Watch* (www.searchenginewatch.com). For this section of this chapter, for example, valuable information about search mechanisms, their indexing methods, and key players was drawn from articles by Danny Sullivan on Search Engine Watch. The number of search engines is growing, but a few of the major players at the time of publication of this book were:

AltaVista www.altavista.com	Opened in 1995 and run by Compaq, it is the largest search engine in terms of number of pages indexed and is a favorite among researchers.
Excite www.excite.com	Opened in 1995, it combined with Magellan and Webcrawler and continues to run them as separate services.
Infoseek infoseek.go.com	Well-known, reviewed, and connected, it expanded in 1996 to 30 million sites.

Lycos www.lycos.com	Begun as a project at Carnegie Mellon University, it provides one of the oldest Web rating services, offering what its editors consider to be the top 5% of websites.
Yahoo www.yahoo.com	Referred to as a meta-search engine, it allows users to search simultaneously any or all of nine search engines.
Profusion profusion.ittc.ukans.edu	In existence since 1994, it is the largest directory, and is well-respected for its carefully selected sites, controlled vocabulary, and links to other search mechanisms.

The type and amount of information available on the Internet today—let's not try to imagine the future—is truly amazing. For example, you can find information about newspapers (www. worldwidenews.com) and about popular magazines (www.path finder.com). You can locate city descriptions (www.usacitylink.com) and Yellow Pages phone directories for selected cities (www. bigyellow.com). You can even search for the names of individuals, their e-mail addresses, and their phone numbers on a service called *People Finder* or *People Search,* located through the search mechanism you select.

Although valuable information about the world of business is still found in print reference works in libraries, a growing number of Internet resources provide company information:

The Big Book www.bigbook.com	Lists name, location, and type of 11 million businesses, including a detailed map with a zoom-in feature to the city block level.

EDGAR www.sec.gov/edgarhp.htm	Provides financial information drawn from Security Exchange Commission (SEC) reports on 3,500 U.S. public corporations and small businesses.
Hoover's Online www.hoovers.com	Contains a "Corporate Directory" with profiles of publicly listed and traded companies, and more than 1,200 of the largest privately held companies, including links to other valuable information resources.
PCQuote www.pcquote.com	Provides stock quotes and market summaries.

As you locate companies, most will have websites with detailed information about their products and services.

If you are seeking information about the federal government, a detailed listing of all of its branches—executive, legislative, and judicial—can be found on the Internet (www. lib.lsu.edu/gov/fedgov.html) through Louisiana State University. Agencies and bureaus are listed as links so that you can move quickly to any part of this vast organization. Listings and links for all branches of the military services also can be found here. Information about professional associations can be found through the Virtual Community of Associations (www.vcanet.org) in their Association Directory.

Your information needs may not be met by any of these sources; these are only examples to let you know about the vast information resources available. Our best advice is explore, explore, explore! Once you have the information you need, think carefully about what you need it for, and how to integrate it with one of the seven ways of learning.

The Internet also has more than static websites. It has mechanisms for communication among people with common interests. Participation in a discussion group enables you to join and enjoy the community aspect of the Internet. Four types of discussion opportunities exist: e-mail, listserves, newsgroups, and live conferencing.

Although *e-mail* is used primarily for asynchronous (at different times) personal communication (similar to sending a letter, but much faster), it is also a great way to communicate with genuine experts. Scholars seldom object to being contacted by e-mail. You can reach them through the home page of their university, their publisher, or a directory of e-mail addresses.

Listserves are essentially e-mail mailing lists, where individuals sign up to participate or are automatically included through membership in an organization. Messages, announcements, or articles posted to a listserve are sent automatically to the people on the list via e-mail. Already nearly 100,000 listserves are available on a broad range of topics.

Newsgroups are similar to listserves but exist through mechanisms independent of e-mail and are housed in various organizations as websites. The terminology varies from system to system—the groups are called *forums* on CompuServe, *conferences* on Peacenet, *meetings* on Ecunet, and *newsgroups* on Usenet—but the concept is the same: people from all around the world with similar interests can share ideas on a designated topic and participate in a discussion by posting their responses.

Usenet, one of the large providers, began in 1979 and now serves over 9,000 topic-specific newsgroups, a number that is growing each day. Originally used by scientists around the world to share research problems and results, newsgroups are now used by scholars, traditional students, adult learners, and the general public in a broad array of fields. These are truly open, democratic forums where any opinion can be posted or responded to, and it is important to recognize this. Discussions are often heated and comments are sometimes hostile and derogatory. An emerging *netiquette* urges *posters* to avoid the senseless name-calling and personal attacks that serve as *flame-bait* and lead to *flame wars*. You need not participate by responding to a posting; you can play the role of *lurker* and just watch the discussion.

How do you find a newsgroup that fits your interests? As with information found in libraries and on websites, there are search mechanisms. Some newsgroups require membership through an organization or professional association for access, but many public newsgroups also exist. Newsgroups are categorized by topics following established conventions for naming them. A newsgroup name generally has three or four parts (hierarchies) in lower case separated by periods, such as alt.business.career-opportunities.executives. The first part describes the general topic level, such as alt. These broad topic areas carry abbreviations such as sci for scientific, comp for computer, soc for society, rec for recreational, news for current events, alt for alternative, and so forth. The next part of the hierarchy takes you to the sub-division of the general topic level, such as business. The remaining parts of the name carry the specific topic, such as career-opportunities.executive. As with other search mechanisms, your key words are matched to the name of the newsgroups that appear to have a close fit. You can search for newsgroups using the major search mechanisms listed above. A special-ized newsgroup search mechanism such as DejaNews (www.dejanews.com) provides certain features that allow you to customize your search, to manage your key words, seek current or older postings, search for concise or detailed postings, and so forth. Depending on the arrangements provided by the mecha-nism you are using, you can respond to the whole newsgroup or only to the author of the posting. If you are looking for a par-ticular newsgroup, or if you intend to start a newsgroup and want to avoid a duplication in naming it, you can review the master list of newsgroup hierarchies, which contains a glossary of abbreviations (www.magma.ca/~leisen/master_list.html).

The Internet also provides live conferencing opportunities involving *synchronous discussion* between or among people logged onto the Internet at the same time. Once connected these people can write messages back and forth much in the way one might talk on the telephone, but at considerably less expense. This capability has led to an arrangement called *chat rooms*, where several people from around the world can hold discussions on a topic of common interest. In recent years, synchronous voice communication has come to be supported by video, so that digitized documents and images also can be sent using the Internet.

If you do not have access to the Internet, check your public library. The Gates Foundation supports Internet access through state library systems.

Time Out

How would you rate yourself as an Internet user on a scale of 1 to 10, where 10 is every week? How would you rate your competence in using the Internet for searching for information on a scale of 1 to 10 where 10 is highly competent? Do you have a good understanding of how to use Internet resources for the information you need most? Do you need practice? Do you need a tutor to help you upgrade your skills?

Managing your own learning also involves integrating information into the learning process in appropriate ways. No other generation has ever had the opportunity to find so much information about so many topics so easily. Just go find it.

BECOMING A PERPETUAL LEARNER

. . . .

Expanding Your Opportunities for Learning

NOW YOU KNOW MOST OF WHAT YOU NEED to know to manage your own learning. You know how to:

- evaluate your previous learning.

- develop a personal plan for needed learning.

- estimate your potential for learning.

- reframe your ideas about learning.

- recognize the value of well-established learning theories.

- be an effective participant in seven different ways of learning.

- select the way of learning that matches your goals for learning.

- maximize learning through appropriate intensity, frequency, and duration.

- assess your learning.

- find the information you need to support your learning.

Two challenges remain:

- to discover opportunities for continuing your learning.

- to find ways to share your learning.

Perpetual learners are constantly seeking to expand their opportunities for learning. They frequently revise their plan for learning. They know where to find resources for formal and informal learning. In this chapter you will find suggestions about how to discover learning opportunities in familiar and unfamiliar places. You will also be encouraged to think about how you can facilitate learning for others and share your learning.

REVISING YOUR PLAN FOR LEARNING
Periodic Reassessment

Recall that your plan for learning was based on an honest examination of your current learning and a careful analysis of needed learning. Your plan also included a gap analysis to identify the discrepancies between current learning and needed learning. When new learning flows into this gap, as it surely will, the gap closes. The old gap is filled, partially or completely, with new learning. Meanwhile, forces within your organization—a job change, a new technology, or new modes of organization—reshape your concept of needed learning. New personal interests and aspirations may also emerge. Perhaps you make a career change or decide to undertake a new course of study. All of these situations provide the occasion for reassessment of your plan for learning. The planning cycle repeats because this is the Age of Perpetual Learning. All you need to do is to go back to your personal plan for learning and build on what you have already accomplished: set new goals, describe the gap, and develop a new action plan.

Time Out

Think back over the important opportunities you have had for learning in your lifetime. How did you find them? Did these opportunities
simply appear? Did you seek them out? What role did friends and
family play? Did you have a mentor or skilled advisor? Could you use
help now in becoming more systematic about your search for opportunities for further learning? Do you know where to look and how to
look?

CONTINUING YOUR LEARNING
Finding the Resources

As you develop and reassess your plan for learning, you face the
challenge of locating additional resources for continuing your
learning. We cannot suggest exactly which resources will be best
for you, but we can show you where to look for them so that
on your own initiative you can find appropriate opportunities for
continuing your learning.

If your plan calls for continuing some aspect of your formal
education and the next step for you is to complete high school,
most community college, military, or high school counselors can
inform you about how to prepare for the test of General Educational Development (GED). If the next level for you is college
or community college, you can explore the programs of different colleges through Peterson's: The Education Supersite
(www.petersons.com). Many colleges and universities now provide bachelor's degree completion programs in accelerated
(weekend or evening) formats. The Peterson's website is also a
valuable resource if the next level for you is graduate or professional education. By selecting the menu option *Pursue Grad-*

uate Programs you can explore more than 35,000 programs by institution or field, including business schools, law schools, and others. A key word search by field will take you to programs around the country and you can then explore, usually through a link (a prearranged connection between websites), the program offered at a particular institution. Formal graduate programs will be found in traditional academic departments, but you may also find degree programs—often with a more "applied" emphasis and special concern for adult learners—in the continuing education or extension divisions of these institutions. Providers of programs for adults usually belong to the University Continuing Education Association (UCEA). If you visit the website for this association, (www.nucea.edu), you will find a state-by-state listing of member institutions, often with direct links to their programs.

If your plan for further learning does not necessarily include a degree program but calls for short-term studies that lead to a certificate, or simply for a course, workshop, or training opportunity, the options available are nearly limitless.

The first place to look is within your own organization. Most organizations have some form of training and development provided through their personnel or human resources division. Look for listings or catalogs of training activities. Some large organizations have corporate universities. Examples include Motorola University, AT&T Learning Center, Disney University, Sears University, and IBM's Global Campus. A comprehensive list of corporate universities is available on a website (www.kwheeler.com) under the *Corporate Education* menu.

You can continue your search for short-term programs, individual courses, or workshops by checking the websites and catalogs of community colleges, four-year colleges, and universities in your region. Some large universities provide extensive continuing education opportunities across metropolitan areas. For example, the University of California at Los Angeles, through

UCLA Extension, provides more than 4,500 programs for adult learners in over fifty locations in the Los Angeles area. In addition, UCLA Extension provides continuing education opportunities for nonresidents (people living outside of California) across the U.S. and worldwide through intensive programs, short-term certificate programs, online courses, and other formats. At the UCLA website (www.ucla.edu/home/continuing.html) you can find more information and a catalog of courses. Other examples with programs comparable to those at UCLA Extension can be found at New York University's School of Continuing and Professional Studies (www.scps.nyu.edu) and University of Minnesota's University College (www.cee.umn.edu).

You do not need to live in a populated metropolitan area to have access to opportunities for adult learners. Multicampus community colleges or state university systems often have programs for adults in rural areas. For example, Colorado Mountain College offers programs at thirteen sites in small towns in the Rocky Mountains west of Denver (www.coloradomtn.edu). The University of Alaska state system provides an extensive network of branch campuses in rural towns and remote areas. A map of those remote areas is available online (info.alaska.edu).

Another avenue for furthering your learning, and one that is increasing in scope and growing in importance today, is the postsecondary sector of proprietary schools, sometimes known as *trade schools.* These include business and secretarial schools, industrial and technical institutes, schools for medical assistants and technicians, art schools, and language schools. Some offer degrees, but most also offer short-term certificate programs or a sequence of related courses. Although these schools are run as for-profit businesses, they are carefully regulated by state and federal agencies and they have their own national, specialized accrediting bodies. If you want to locate these schools, begin by looking under *schools* in the Yellow Pages of your phone directory or on the Internet for Yellow Pages in other cities. If you want to check on accreditation status, contact one or the other of two national accrediting bodies: Accrediting Council for Independent Colleges and Schools, or Accrediting Commission of Career Schools and Colleges of Technology.

Many professional associations also set standards and provide opportunities for continuing education. For example, in business the American Management Association (www.mce.be) offers courses, multiday public workshops, and onsite customized training. Opportunities are made available around the world through the Global Training Resources Program. In addition, self-study training and development programs in print, audio-cassette/workbook, and CD-ROM formats are offered. For attorneys, the American Bar Association (ABA) provides resources for continuing education. The ABA website (www.abanet.org) provides a list of all state requirements for continuing legal education (CLE) and an online catalog. For health professionals, such as nurses or physician assistants, standards for continuing medical education (CME) are set by various professional bodies that also control certification. Opportunities for further education are found at large university health sciences centers, at local hospitals and clinics, and through private companies that conduct CME as a business. CME opportunities are also available at local, state, and national conventions of professional bodies, and these are often sponsored by pharmaceutical companies. If you are engaged in a type of work that might be defined broadly as a profession, seek out the standards and learning opportunities of that profession.

If you work in a business, particularly a small business, you might want to seek training and development opportunities through various business affiliations such as local chambers of commerce. A website called *Online Chambers* (online-chamber.com) provides state, national, and international listings, and links to local chambers of commerce with their lists of courses and workshops. Another website called *The Training*

Registry (www.tregistry.com) provides menus of courses, providers, and local listings for training opportunities in your area.

If your schedule does not permit going to a college campus or other site for classes, you may want to explore the growing number of distance learning arrangements that make it possible to study at home or the workplace. *Distance learning,* also called *distributed learning,* uses various formats to connect students and instructors. For example, the distance learning division of Indiana University lists several delivery systems, including independent study courses, videoconferencing, Internet, satellite, videotape, broadcast/cable, and two-way audio and video instruction at remote sites. If you return to the Peterson's website mentioned earlier, you will find distance learning programs by subject area (www.petersons.com/dlearn) and these will give you the college and university sponsors. If you are interested only in web-based course materials, you can search through *World Lecture Hall* (www.utexas.edu/world/lecture) to find a list by field of courses created by faculty worldwide who are using the Web to deliver class materials.

Distance learning opportunities are likely to expand significantly in the years just ahead, as computer and software companies create partnerships with universities. For example, Lucent Technologies (www.lucent.com/cedl) through its Center for Excellence in Distance Learning (CEDL) is already working with recognized distance education providers such as Indiana University, Penn State University, and the University of Wisconsin-Extension.

Not all distance learning is through university-based providers. A fast-growing area of educational opportunity is commercial Internet education. Companies are now creating online universities that offer courses for a fee. One example is Ziff-Davis University, which offers online courses as part of its broader activity in publishing magazines and managing trade shows. For a monthly fee, subscribers to ZDU (www.zdu.com) can take an unlimited number of courses, mainly to develop information technology skills. Another example is Jones International University (http://www.international.edu/home.html), which markets itself as "The University of the Web."

In addition to these structured and semistructured opportunities for continuing your learning, many informal arrangements for learning exist in familiar places such as local museums, zoos, historic sites, churches, clubs, factories, medical centers, symphonies, theaters, and other not-for-profit organizations. In recent years these organizations have become quite expert at providing user-friendly exhibits, tours, short courses, and workshops. Although one might think of plays and films primarily as entertainment, at another level there is much to be learned from them, particularly about other countries, cultures, and periods of history. Independent bookstores and many of the new bookstore chains now offer inviting environments for browsing (complete with coffee bar), and many carry good collections of foreign magazines and newspapers, audiocassettes, CDs, and software. If you are too busy to visit a bookstore or library, you can seek sources of electronic books (www.kbc.com/html/-ebooks.htm) or subscribe to an electronic book service and download "e-books" to your laptop so you can read as you commute or travel.

We are witnessing a worldwide revolution in access to adult learning opportunities that is both a cause and result of the Information Age. These expanding opportunities for learning have become an essential feature of the new era. If you want to learn something—almost anything—there are providers eager to teach you. Perpetual learners actively seek out these opportunities.

Time Out

Let's look ahead. What are you going to do with your new learning? Is it simply for your personal use, or do you plan to share it?

LEADERSHIP FOR LEARNING
Sharing What You Know

As you develop skill in managing your own learning, you will not only become better at learning but you will actually learn more. You may even feel a newfound joy in learning. Then you will *want* to learn more. Success breeds success. Certain natural consequences flow from your growing expertise and satisfaction as a learner. Your new learning provides you with improved performance and expanded capacity. As the cycle of perpetual learning continues you are given new opportunities and you are challenged again with new learning.

In addition, as a person with emerging expertise in learning you may have the occasion to help someone else with their learning, or perhaps even serve as someone's mentor. When training and development experiences are being planned, you can make a significant contribution by representing the interests of participants in that process. You can identify learning outcomes and suggest what ways of learning should be given consideration. These may be new roles for you, but you can gain unexpected satisfactions from providing leadership for learning.

Furthermore, you may even become so interested in the process of learning that you want to explore the role of facilitator. If so, you can learn more about the facilitator's role in learning from the companion to this book, *Effective Training Strategies: A Comprehensive Guide to Maximizing Learning in Organizations* (Davis and Davis, 1998).[1] Standing beside the natural learner in most of us is the eager teacher waiting to be born. One important way to further your learning is to try to teach what you know to someone else. In fact, teaching someone what you have learned is one of the best ways to learn. We might even think of it as an eighth way of learning.

One of the key challenges in the learning organization is to get people to share their knowledge. There is a tendency to hoard what we know, protecting our own little competitive advantage by knowing what nobody else knows. We have all met people who maintain their position, sometimes even terrorizing people of lesser rank, through the power of their knowledge. Francis Bacon was right: knowledge is power. On the other hand, knowledge becomes even more powerful when it is shared. What makes an organization strong is shared knowledge. What makes a civilization strong is accumulated wisdom.

Organizations that aspire to become effective learning organizations are not only interested in stimulating individual learning for all employees, they also want to develop mechanisms for sharing that learning. This is why they are talking about *knowledge management* and appointing *chief learning officers*. What they are encountering is a huge inertia about sharing. The two favorite excuses they identify are: "I didn't know someone else needed this information," and "I didn't know so-and-so knew about that." Some organizations are rearranging physical space to foster better communication, some are developing learning communities around identified interests, and others are investing heavily in computer systems for saving, retrieving, and sharing information. All of these efforts are creating organizational cultures where sharing knowledge is highly valued. Not only is perpetual learning an expectation in most organizations today, shared learning is also a necessity. It makes sense if you realize that we are truly living in a new era, where knowledge is the most important natural resource.

We hope that the ultimate byproduct of all this individual learning and shared knowledge is a better world. We all need organizations that are more efficient and effective, workers and volunteers who take pride in and find joy in their daily tasks, and leaders who are inspiring. We need lively colleagues, and we ourselves need to be stimulating companions to those around us. Whatever you may believe about the ultimate progress of civilization, the new era and the new century provide promising opportunities for a better way of life.

The new era of rapid change plays to the greatest strength of human beings: adaptability. The squirrel will always gather nuts by instinct and the beaver will always build its house in the same way. Humans are the learning species, the fittest to learn. We can adapt to rapid change by constantly seeking ways to expand our opportunities for learning. Even more important, we are capable of developing our varied talents to the fullest and dreaming dreams of what might be.

NOTES
· · · · · · · · · ·

Introduction

1. Stewart, Thomas A. and Jane Furth. (1994, April 4). "The Information Age in Charts." *Fortune, 129:7,* pp. 75–80.

2. Ibid.

3. Toffler, Alvin. 1980. *The Third Wave.* New York: William Morrow, p. 20.

4. ———. 1970. *Future Shock.* New York: Random House, p. 13.

5. Ibid., pp. 20–34.

6. ———. 1972. *The Futurists.* New York: Random House.

7. Davis, James and Adelaide Davis. 1998. *Effective Training Strategies: A Comprehensive Guide to Maximizing Learning in Organizations.* San Francisco: Berrett-Koehler.

Chapter 1. Taking Charge

1. Weingartner, Rudolph. 1992. *Undergraduate Education: Goals and Means.* Phoenix: The Oryx Press and The American Council on Education.

Chapter 2. Knowing Yourself as a Learner

1. Levinson, Daniel F. 1996. *The Seasons of a Woman's Life.* New York: Ballantine Books.

2. Havinghurst, Robert. 1972. *Developmental Tasks and Education.* New York: Longman.

3. Sheehy, Gail. 1995. *New Passages: Mapping Your Life Across Time*. New York: Random House.

4. Sternberg, Robert. 1985. *Beyond IQ: A Triarchic Theory of Intelligence*. New York: Cambridge University Press.

5. Gardner, Howard. 1983. *Frames of Mind: The Theory of Multiple Intelligences*. New York: Basic Books.

6. Woldkowski, Raymond. 1993. *Enhancing Adult Motivation to Learn*. San Francisco: Jossey-Bass.

7. Bandura, A. 1986. *Social Foundations of Thought and Action: A Social Cognitive Theory*. Upper Saddle River, NJ: Prentice-Hall.

Chapter 3. Redefining Learning

1. Argyris, Chris. 1991. *Harvard Business Review*. Reprint 91301, pp. 1–15.

2. Shenk, David. 1997. *Data Smog: Surviving the Information Glut*. San Francisco: HarperEdge.

3. Barrett, Neil. 1997. *The State of Cybernation*. London: Kogan Page Limited, pp. 34–58.

4. Freire, Paulo. 1987. *Pedagogy of the Oppressed*. New York: Continuum, p. 58.

5. Weingartner, Rudolph. 1992. *Undergraduate Education: Goals and Means*. Phoenix: The Oryx Press and The American Council on Education, pp. 104–5.

6. Postman, Neil and Charles Weingartner. 1969. *Teaching as a Subversive Activity*. New York: Delacourte Press, p. 21.

Part Two: Introduction to the Seven Ways of Learning

1. Morrow, Alfred. 1969. *The Practical Theorist: The Life and Work of Kurt Lewin*. New York: Basic Books.

2. Davis, James and Adelaide Davis. 1998. *Effective Training Strategies: A Comprehensive Guide to Maximizing Learning in Organizations*. San Francisco: Berrett-Koehler, pp. 91–92.

Chapter 4. Learning New Skills

1. Skinner, B.F. 1953. *Science and Human Behavior*. New York: Free Press.

2. ———. 1974. *About Behaviorism*. New York: Knopf.

3. Keller, Fred S. 1969. *Learning: Reinforcement Theory,* 2nd ed. New York: Random House.

4. Mager, Robert E. 1962. *Preparing Instructional Objectives*. Palo Alto, CA: Fearon.

5. Davis, Robert, Lawrence T. Alexander and Stephen L. Yelon. 1974. *Learning System Design*. New York: McGraw-Hill.

6. Bandura, Albert. 1969. *Principles of Behavior Modification*. New York: Holt, Rinehart, and Winston.

7. Skinner, B.F. 1961. "Why We Need Teaching Machines" *Harvard Educational Review, 31,* pp. 377–98.

8. Graham, Neill. 1986. *The Mind Tool: Computers and Their Impact on Society*. St. Paul, MN: West Publishing.

9. McCann, P. 1981. "Learning Strategies and Computer-Based Instruction." *Computers and Education, 5:3,* pp. 133–40.

10. Keller, Fred. 1968. "Good-bye Teacher." *Journal of Applied Behavioral Analysis, 1,* pp. 79–88.

Chapter 5. Learning From Presentations

1. Gardner, Howard. 1985. *The Mind's New Science: A History of the Cognitive Revolution*. New York: Basic Books.

2. Neisser, Ulrich. 1967. *Cognitive Psychology*. New York: Appleton-Century-Crofts.

3. Atkinson, R.C. and R.M. Shiffran. 1968. "Human Memory: A Proposed System and Its Control Processes" in K.W. Spence and T.W. Spence (eds.). *The Psychology of Learning and Motivation,* vol. 2. New York: Academic Press.

4. Cherry, C. 1957. *On Human Communication*. New York: Wiley.

5. Broadbent, D.E. 1958. *Perception and Communication*. London: Pergammon Press.

6. Lindsey, P. and D. Norman. 1972. *Human Information Processing: An Introduction to Psychology*. New York: Academic Press.

7. Triesman, A.M. 1960. "Contextual Cues in Encoding Listening." *Quarterly Journal of Experimental Psychology, 12,* pp. 242–8.

8. Shiffran, R.M. and N. Schneider. 1977. "Controlled and Automatic Human Information Processing II. Perceptual Learning, Automatic Attending, and a General Theory." *Psychological Review, 84,* pp. 127–190.

9. Sanford, Anthony J. 1985. *Cognition and Cognitive Psychology*. New York: Basic Books.

10. Zimbardo, Phillip. 1985. *Psychology and Life*. Glenview, IL: Scott, Foresman.

11. Sanford, Anthony J. 1985. *Cognition and Cognitive Psychology*. New York: Basic Books.

12. Loftus, Elizabeth. 1980. *Memory*. Reading, MA: Addison-Wesley.

13. Sanford, Anthony J. 1985. *Cognition and Cognitive Psychology*. New York: Basic Books.

14. Shepherd, R.N. 1967. "Recognition Memory for Words, Sentences, and Pictures." *Journal of Verbal Learning, 6,* pp. 156–63.

15. Lorayne, H. and J. Lucas, 1974. *The Memory Book*. New York: Stein & Day.

16. Loftus, Elizabeth. 1980. *Memory*. Reading, MA: Addison-Wesley.

17. Pompi, K.F. and R. Lachman. 1967. "Surrogate Processes in the Short-Term Retention of Connected Discourse." *Journal of Experimental Psychology, 75,* pp. 143–50.

Chapter 6. Learning to Think

1. Paul, Richard. 1995. *Critical Thinking*. Santa Rosa, CA: Foundation for Critical Thinking, p. 113.

2. Glaser, Edward. 1941. *An Experiment in the Development of Critical Thinking*. New York: AMS Press.

3. Guilford, J.P. 1986. *Creative Talents*. Buffalo, NY: Bearly Limited.

4. Torrence, E. Paul. 1995. *Why Fly?* Norwood, NJ: Ablex.

5. Halpern, Diane. 1984. *Thought and Knowledge: An Introduction to Critical Thinking*. Hillsdale, NJ: Erlbaum.

6. Ennis, Robert. 1987. "A Taxonomy of Critical Thinking Dispositions and Abilities" in Joan Baron and Robert Sternberg (eds.) *Teaching Thinking Skills*. New York: Wilt Freeman.

7. Beyer, Barry. 1985. *Practical Strategies for the Teaching of Thinking*. Hillsdale, NJ: Earlbaum, p. 19.

8. Kurfiss, Joanne. 1988. *Critical Thinking*. Washington, D.C.: Association for the Study of Higher Education, p. 2.

9. Beyer, Barry. 1985. *Practical Strategies for the Teaching of Thinking*. Hillsdale, NJ: Earlbaum, p. 33.

10. Paul, Richard. 1987. "Dialogical Thinking: Critical Thought Essential to the Acquisition of Rational Knowledge and Passions" in Joan Baron and Robert Sternberg (eds.) p. 128. *Teaching Thinking Skills*. New York: Wilt Freeman.

11. Nickerson, Raymond, David Perkins and Edward Smith. 1985. *The Teaching of Thinking*. Hillsdale, NJ: Erlbaum.

12. Ibid., 44.

13. Beyer, Barry. 1985. *Practical Strategies for the Teaching of Thinking*. Hillsdale, NJ: Earlbaum, pp. 20, 25.

14. Nickerson, Raymond. 1986. *Reflections on Reasoning*. Hillsdale, NJ: Erlbaum, p. 35.

15. Ibid., p. 20.

16. Schwarze, Sharon and Harvey Lape. 1997. *Thinking Socratically.* Upper Sadle River, NJ: Prentice-Hall, pp. 49–50.

17. Nickerson, Raymond. 1986. *Reflections on Reasoning.* Hillsdale, NJ: Erlbaum, p. 68.

18. Browne, M. Neil and Stuart Keeley. 1994. *Asking the Right Questions.* Englewood Cliffs, NJ: Prentice-Hall, p. 16.

19. Nickerson, Raymond. 1986. *Reflections on Reasoning.* Hillsdale, NJ: Erlbaum, 36.

20. Ibid., 36.

21. Corbett, Edward. 1991. *The Elements of Reasoning.* New York: Macmillan, pp. 11–46.

22. Ibid., pp. 42–45.

23. Ibid., pp. 21–23.

24. Halpern, Diane. 1984. *Thought and Knowledge: An Introduction to Critical Thinking.* Hillsdale, NJ: Erlbaum, p. 27.

25. Corbett, Edward. 1991. *The Elements of Reasoning.* New York: Macmillan.

26. Browne, M. Neil and Stuart Keeley. 1994. *Asking the Right Questions.* Englewood Cliffs, NJ: Prentice-Hall.

27. Nickerson, Raymond. 1986. *Reflections on Reasoning.* Hillsdale, NJ: Erlbaum.

28. Weisberg, Robert. 1993. *Beyond the Myth of Genius.* New York: Frieman.

29. Guilford, J.P. 1986. *Creative Talents.* Buffalo, NY: Bearly Limited, pp. 41–50.

30. Baer, John. 1993. *Creativity and Divergent Thinking: A Task-Specific Approach.* Hillsdale, NJ: Erlbaum.

31. Csikszentmihalyi, Mihaly. 1996. *Creativity: Flow and the Psychology of Discovery and Invention.* New York: HarperCollins, pp. 79–80.

32, Ibid.

33. Paul, Richard. 1987. "Dialogical Thinking: Critical Thought Essential to the Acquisition of Rational Knowledge and Passions" in Joan Baron and Robert Sternberg (eds.) *Teaching Thinking Skills.* New York: Wilt Freeman, p. 292.

34. Ibid., p. 258.

35. Ibid., pp. 259–262.

36. Ibid., p. 138.

37. Ibid., p. 297.

38. Dillon, J.T. 1990. *The Practice of Questioning.* London: Routledge.

Chapter 7. Learning to Solve Problems and Make Decisions

1. Fixx, J.F. 1978. *Solve It*. New York: Doubleday.

2. Bransford, John and Barry Stein. 1993. *The Ideal Problem Solver: A Guide for Improving Thinking, Learning, and Creativity*. New York: Freeman, pp. 8–9.

3. Ward, Thomas, Ronald Finke, and Steven Smith. 1995. *Creativity and the Mind: Discovering the Genius Within*. New York: Plenum Press, p. 53.

4. Glucksberg, Sam. 1988. "Language and Thought" in Robert Sternberg and Edward Smith (eds.), *The Psychology of Human Thought*. New York: Cambridge University Press, based on work by S.M. Kosslyn. 1983. *Ghosts in the Mind's Machine*. New York: Norton.

5. Dworetzky, John. 1985. *Psychology*, 2nd ed. New York: West Publishing, pp. 237–38.

6. Dellarosa, Denise. 1988. "A History of Thinking" in Robert Sternberg and Edward Smith (eds.), *The Psychology of Human Thought*. New York: Cambridge University Press.

7. Newell, Allan and Herbert A. Simon. 1972. *Human Problem-Solving*. Englewood Cliffs, NJ: Prentice Hall.

8. Baron, Jonathan. 1994. *Thinking and Deciding*. New York: Cambridge University Press, p. 315.

9. Newell, Allan and Herbert A. Simon. 1972. *Human Problem-Solving*. Englewood Cliffs, NJ: Prentice Hall, pp. 53–63, 787–91.

10. Halpern, Diane. 1984. *Thought and Knowledge: An Introduction to Critical Thinking*. Hillsdale, NJ: Erlbaum, p. 189.

11. Baron, Jonathan. 1994. *Thinking and Deciding*. New York: Cambridge University Press, p. 68.

12. Halpern, Diane. 1984. *Thought and Knowledge: An Introduction to Critical Thinking*. Hillsdale, NJ: Erlbaum, pp. 182–4.

13. Ibid., pp. 184–5.

14. Ibid., pp. 192–3.

15. Wickelgren, Wayne. 1974. *How to Solve Problems: Elements of a Theory of Problems and Problem Solving*. San Francisco: Freeman, pp. 46–47.

16. Ibid., p. 26.

17. Ibid., pp. 109–10.

18. Halpern, Diane. 1984. *Thought and Knowledge: An Introduction to Critical Thinking*. Hillsdale, NJ: Erlbaum, pp. 167–74.

19. Holyoak, Keith J. and Richard Nesbitt. 1988. "Induction" in Robert Sternberg and Edward Smith (eds.), *The Psychology of Human Thought*. New York: Cambridge University Press, pp. 82–3.

20. Sanford, Anthony J. 1985. *Cognition and Cognitive Psychology*. New York: Basic Books, p. 46.

21. Glucksberg, Sam. 1988. "Language and Thought" in Robert Sternberg and Edward Smith (eds.), *The Psychology of Human Thought* (p. 225). New York: Cambridge University Press, based on work by S.M. Kosslyn. 1983. *Ghosts in the Mind's Machine.* New York: Norton.

22. Halpern, Diane. 1984. *Thought and Knowledge: An Introduction to Critical Thinking*. Hillsdale, NJ: Erlbaum, pp. 1–5.

23. Ibid., pp. 221–22.

24. Ibid., p. 222ff.

25. Baron, Jonathan. 1994. *Thinking and Deciding*. New York: Cambridge University Press, pp. 246–49.

26. Halpern, Diane. 1984. *Thought and Knowledge: An Introduction to Critical Thinking*. Hillsdale, NJ: Erlbaum, p. 123.

27. Baron, Jonathan. 1994. *Thinking and Deciding*. New York: Cambridge University Press, pp. 229–30.

28. Halpern, Diane. 1984. *Thought and Knowledge: An Introduction to Critical Thinking*. Hillsdale, NJ: Erlbaum, p. 23ff.

29. Pigors, Paul and Faith Pigors, 1987. "Case Method" in Robert L. Craig (ed.), *Training and Development Handbook: A Guide to Human Resource Development,* 3rd ed. New York: McGraw-Hill, p. 415.

30. Leenders, Michiel and James Erskine. 1973. *Case Research: The Case Writing Process*. London, Ontario, Canada: The University of Western Ontario, p. 110.

31. Pigors, Paul and Faith Pigors, 1987. "Case Method" in Robert L. Craig (ed.), *Training and Development Handbook: A Guide to Human Resource Development,* 3rd ed. New York: McGraw-Hill, pp. 415–19.

32. Barnes, Louis B., C. Roland Christiansen and Abby J. Hansen. 1994. *Teaching and the Case Method*. Boston, MA: Harvard Business School Press, p. 46.

Chapter 8. Learning in Groups

1. Hare, A. Paul. 1976. "The History and Present State of Small Group Research" in *Handbook of Small Group Research,* 2nd ed. New York: Free Press.

2. Lorge, Irvin. 1958. "A Survey of the Studies Contrasting the Quality of Group Performance and Individual Performance." *Psychological Bulletin, 55:332,* p. 72.

3. Berelson, Bernard and Gary Steiner. 1964. *Human Behavior: An Inventory of Scientific Findings.* New York: Harcourt, Brace & World.

4. Larson, Carl and Frank LaFasto. 1989. *Teamwork: What Must Go Right/What Can Go Wrong.* London: Sage Publications.

5. Goldberg, Alvin, and Carl Larson. 1975. *Group Communication.* Englewood Cliffs, NJ: Prentice-Hall.

6. Barker, Larry L., Kathy J. Wahlers, Kittie W. Watson, and Robert J. Kibler. 1987. *Groups in Process: An Introduction to Small Group Communication,* 3rd ed. Englewood Cliffs, NJ: Prentice-Hall.

7. Benne, Kenneth D. and Paul Sheets. 1948. "Functional Roles of Group Members." *Journal of Social Issues.* (Spring): pp. 41–49.

8. Tuckman, Bruce W. 1965. "Developmental Sequence in Small Groups." *Psychological Bulletin, 63,* pp. 384–99.

9. Fisher, B. Aubrey. 1980. *Small Group Decision Making.* New York: McGraw-Hill.

10. Kelly, Charles M. 1970. "Empathic Listening." Robert S. Cathcart and Larry A. Samovar. *Small Group Communication: A Reader.* Dubuque, IA: Brown.

11. Baird, John E., Jr., and Sanford Weinberg. 1970. "Elements of Group Communication." Robert S. Cathcart and Larry H. Samovar. *Small Group Communication: A Reader.* Dubuque, IA: Brown.

12. Bradford, Leland, Dorothy Stock, and Murray Horowitz. 1970. "How to Diagnose Group Problems." Robert Golembiewski and Arthur Blumberg, (eds.), *Sensitivity Training and the Laboratory Approach.* Itasca, IL: Peacock Publishers.

13. Fisher, B. Aubrey. 1980. *Small Group Decision Making: Communications and the Group Process.* New York: McGraw Hill, p. 54.

14. Janis, Irvin. 1972. *Victims of Groupthink: A Psychological Study of Foreign Policy Decisions and Fiascos.* Boston: Houghton Mifflin.

15. Pavitt, Charles, and Ellen Curtis. 1990. *Small Group Discussion.* Scottsdale, AZ: Gorsuch Scarisbrick.

16. Rogers, Carl. 1970. *Carl Rogers on Encounter Groups.* New York: Harper and Row.

17. Yalom, Irvin D. 1985. *The Theory and Practice of Group Psychotherapy,* 3rd ed. New York: Basic Books.

18. Larson, Carl and Frank LaFasto. 1989. *Teamwork: What Must Go Right/What Can Go Wrong.* London: Sage Publications.

19. Ibid., pp. 39–58.

Chapter 9. Improving Performance

1. Moore, Omar and Alan Anderson 1975. "Some Principles for the Design of Clarifying Educational Environments" in Cathy Greenblatt and Richard Duke (eds.), *Gaming-Simulation: Rationale, Design, and Applications* (pp. 49–50). New York: Wiley.

2. Marineau, Rene. 1989. *Jacob Levy Moreno, 1889–1974: Father of Psychodrama, Sociometry, and Group Psychotherapy.* London: Tavistock/Routledge, pp. 25–49.

3. Jones, Ken. 1987. *Simulations: A Handbook for Teachers and Trainers.* London: Kogan Page.

4. Persell, Caroline. 1989. *Understanding Society: An Introduction to Sociology.* New York: Harper and Row, p. 58.

5. Shaw, M.E., R.J. Corsinni, R.R. Blake, and S.J. Mouton. 1979. "Role Playing" in J.E. Jones and S.W. Pfeiffer (eds.) *The 1979 Annual Handbook for Group Facilitators.* San Diego: University Associates.

6. Cooke, Phyliss. 1987. "Role Playing" in Robert L. Craig (ed.) pp. 430–31. *Training and Development Handbook: A Guide to Human Resource Development,* 3rd ed. New York: McGraw-Hill.

7. Maier, Norman, Allen Solem, and Ayesha Maier. 1975. *The Role-Play Technique.* La Jolla: CA: University Associates, p. 12.

8. Sternberg, Patricia and Antonina Garcia. 1989. *Sociodrama: Who's in Your Shoes?* New York: Praeger.

9. Ibid.

10. Marineau, Rene. 1989. *Jacob Levy Moreno, 1889-1974: Father of Psychodrama, Sociometry, and Group Psychotherapy.* London: Tavistock/Routledge.

11. Sternberg, Patricia and Antonina Garcia. 1989. *Sociodrama: Who's in Your Shoes?* New York: Praeger.

12. Ibid., pp. 55–69.

13. Barton, Richard. 1970. *A Primer on Simulation and Gaming.* Englewood-Cliffs, NJ: Prentice-Hall.

14. Dukes, Richard, and Constance Seidner. 1978. *Learning with Simulations and Games.* Newbury Park, CA: Sage.

15. Abt, Clark. 1970. *Serious Games.* Worthington, OH: University Press of America.

16. Davis, James and Adelaide Davis. 1998. *Effective Training Strategies: A Comprehensive Guide to Maximizing Learning in Organizations.* San Francisco: Berrett-Koehler.

17. Jones, Ken. 1987. *Simulations: A Handbook for Teachers and Trainers.* London: Kogan Page.

Chapter 10. Learning From Experience

1. Flake, Carol (ed.). 1993. *Holistic Education: Principles, Perspectives, and Practices.* Brandon, VT: Holistic Education Press.

2. Gang, Phil. 1993. "Experiential Education" in Carol Flake (ed.), *Holistic Education: Principles, Perspectives, and Practices.* Brandon, VT: Holistic Education Press.

3. Hendley, Brian and Russell Dewey. 1986. *Whitehead: Philosophers as Educators.* Carbondale: Southern Illinois University.

4. Kolb, David. 1984. *Experiential Learning.* Englewood Cliffs, NJ: Prentice-Hall, pp. 22–23.

5. Schön, Donald. 1983. *The Reflective Practitioner: How Professionals Think in Action.* New York: Basic Books.

6. MacLean, Paul D. 1973. *A Triune Concept of the Brain and Behavior.* Toronto, Canada: University of Toronto Press.

7. Sagan, Carl. 1977. *The Dragons of Eden: Speculations on the Evolution of Human Intelligence.* New York: Ballantine Books.

8. Ibid., pp. 53, 57.

9. Ibid., p. 35.

10. Jerison, Harry. 1977. "Evolution of the Brain" in M.C. Wittrock (ed.), *The Human Brain* (p. 42ff). Englewood Cliffs, NJ: Prentice Hall.

11. Fishbach, Gerald. 1994. "Mind and Brain." *A Scientific American Special Report.* New York: Freeman.

12. Sylwester, Robert. 1995. *A Celebration of Neurons: An Educator's Guide to the Human Brain.* Alexandria, VA: Association for Supervision and Curriculum Development.

13. Hart, Leslie. 1983. *Human Brain and Human Learning.* New York: Longman.

14. Smith, Frank. 1990. *To Think.* New York: Teachers College Press.

15. Ibid., p. 12.

16. Hart, Leslie. 1983. *Human Brain and Human Learning.* New York: Longman, p. 109.

17. Smith, Frank. 1990. *To Think.* New York: Teachers College Press, p. 126.

18. Brooks, Jacqueline Grennon and Martin G. Brooks. 1993. *In Search of Understanding: The Case for Constructivist Classrooms.* Alexandria, VA: Association for Supervision and Curriculum Development.

19. Fosnot, Catherine Twomey. 1996. "Constructivism: A Psychological Theory of Learning" in Fosnot (ed.). *Constructivism: Theory, Perspectives, and Practice.* New York: Teachers College Press, pp. 13–14.
20. Egan, Gerard. 1990. *The Skilled Helper: A Systematic Approach to Effective Helping,* 4th ed. Pacific Grove, CA: Brooks/Cole.

Chapter 11. High-Impact Learning

1. Kirkpatrick, Donald. 1996. *Evaluating Training Programs: The Four Levels.* San Francisco: Berrett-Koehler.

Chapter 13. Becoming a Perpetual Learner

1. Davis, James and Adelaide Davis. 1998. *Effective Training Strategies: A Comprehensive Guide to Maximizing Learning in Organizations.* San Francisco: Berrett-Koehler.

INDEX
· · · · · · · · ·

brain structure and, 152–54
constructing meaning, 155,
    157–58
defined, 149–50
facilitators, 157–59
reflection-in-action, 151
reflection process, 156–59
Holyoak, Keith J., 106
Hoover's Online, 185
hope, 132
*Human Brain and Human
    Learning* (Hart), 153
Human Problem Solving (Newell
    and Simon), 101
human relations, 119
hybrid search engines, 182
hypotheses, 89

I

ICOLCC (International Coalition
    of Library Consortia), 178–79
ideas
    collaborative learning and, 119
    fluency of, 93
    holistic learning and, 159
    imagery, 78, 79, 80, 137
    mental models and, 100–101
    pictorial memory, 78
imitation, 59, 132
improving performance. *see* role
    plays; virtual realities
incubation, 93
independent learners, 2
index, as search mechanism, 7
Indiana University, 195
inductive arguments, 89
informal education, 13–14, 196
information, 36–38, 132, 175–77.
    see also sources of information
    access to, 36
    amount of, 36
    packaging, 36
Information Age, 1, 2–3, 36, 43
information giver, 123

information processing, 69, 72–76.
    see also cognitive learning for,
    75–76
information seeker, 123
Infoseek, 183
inherited genius, 92–93
initial state, 102, 114
inquiry learning, 50, 83–98, 171,
    176. *see also* thinking;
    questions
    critical thinking, 83, 85, 87–92,
        170
    dialogical thinking, 42, 85–86,
        95–96, 171
    framing questions, 96–98
    practice, 86
    thinking, 18, 85, 92–95, 170–71
instructional design, 56, 64–65
instrument, 121
integration, 155
intellectual work, 83–84
intelligence, 25, 86, 92–93
intensity, 166–68
interdisciplinary fields, 18
interests, 16
    career paths, 17
    favorite learning experiences, 17
    leisure time, 17
International Coalition of Library
    Consortia (ICOLC), 178–79
Internet, 37, 65, 177, 180–88. *see
    also* World Wide Web
    company information, 184–85
    discussion groups, 185–88
    search mechanisms, 181–83
    URLs, 181
interpersonal learning, 132
interpretations, 72–73, 75, 155,
    156–57
involvement, 94, 113, 122–23
Irskine, James, 112

J

Janis, Irvin, 130

ABOUT THE AUTHORS

J AMES R. DAVIS is a Professor of higher education and adult studies at the University of Denver. He holds degrees from Oberlin College and Yale University and a Ph.D. from Michigan State University in higher education administration. Jim teaches courses on characteristics of adult learners, training, teaching adults, program planning and administration, leadership, and the uses of technology in instruction. He has served in numerous administrative posts, including assistant to the provost, director of the center for academic quality, director of the school of education—all at the University of Denver—and as academic dean at the historically black college, Wilberforce University, Wilberforce, Ohio.

Jim is the author of five other books, the most recent being *Effective Training Strategies: A Comprehensive Guide to Maximizing Learning in Organizations* (1998) with his wife Adelaide B. Davis. He also wrote *Better Teaching, More Learning: Strategies for Success in Postsecondary Settings* (1993) and *Interdisciplinary Courses and Team Teaching: New Arrangements for Learning* (1995). Both books are part of the American Council on Education's Higher Education Series and are published by The Oryx Press in Phoenix, Arizona. As a result of this writing, Jim has served as a consultant to organizations, an invited presenter at conferences, and a workshop leader across the United States and around the world. In 1999 he was a presenter at the annual meetings of the American Society for Training and Development (ASTD) and the International Society for Performance Improvement (ISPI). "I love to help people learn about learning," says Jim, "and I know that most people have room to grow in becoming more effective and efficient learners."

A DELAIDE B. DAVIS served as a training analyst to COPASA MG, a government-sponsored public water and sanitation company in Brazil. She taught human resources management at the Universidade Federal de Minas Gerais in Belo Horizonte, where she also earned her masters degree in administration with a specialization in human resource management. She planned and facilitated numerous training workshops for her company and spoke at several conferences and annual meetings in Brazil.

Adelaide has created a second profession for herself since moving to the United States in 1991, consulting regularly as a software translator and editor for J.D. Edwards World Source Company (Denver) and Sykes Enterprises, Inc. (Boulder) and as a translator in the local county courts. She teaches Portuguese at University College, University of Denver, and is an adjunct Professor of Portuguese at the Colorado School of Mines. She is also the co-author of *Effective Training Strategies: A Comprehensive Guide to Maximizing Learning in Organizations* (1998). "The ultimate training and travel experience for me," notes Adelaide, "was to present (in English) a workshop on teamwork to women faculty members in the college of business at King Abdulaziz University in Jeddah, Saudi Arabia."

Jim and Adelaide like to work together. *Managing Your Own Learning* is their second joint venture as authors, and they have also collaborated as workshop planners and presenters, the most challenging being a bilingual presentation on training strategies for FIAT in Belo Horizonte, Brazil, and a similar arrangement on the topic of teamwork in Brasilia.

Jim and Adelaide hope to focus their time and energies on helping people to learn about learning, not only facilitators of training, but also participants in learning. "We believe that there is a huge gap in understanding," Jim notes, "between what teachers and trainers are doing as facilitators, on the one hand, and what learners could be doing, on the other hand, to maximize their learning." Jim and Adelaide like to help people in organizations get a better grasp of how to use standard, well-researched theories of learning in designing training; but they are also interested in helping adult learners, wherever they may be, to get the most out of the learning experiences they are having. They are available for consulting, speaking, and facilitating workshops on training and managing learning.